More praise for *The Wildlife Watcher*.

"The bountiful wildlife of the southland as lovingly seen and described through the eyes of an adopted son of the South."

CHARLIE DANIELS, country music artist

"Rob writes the kind of book you end up reading in one sitting."

SEAN DIETRICH, writer, "Sean of the South"

"I loooove this book! I was just thinking, I'd give anything to sit down and talk to my grandfather again. This book is like having that opportunity! My Mom's gonna love it, too."

Lee Ann Womack, award-winning country music artist

"An excellent guidebook. Any nature writer who can turn house flies and carpenter bees into must-read stories is worth paying attention to."

SAM VENABLE, columnist, Knoxville (TN) *News Sentinel*

"When I heard Rob was writing a book about the "critters" in the outdoors, I was really excited, and I was not disappointed—what a fun read! This book gave me new perspectives and fresh knowledge about creatures I'm very familiar with. Sometimes I forget that other people see them in different places and in different ways. This is a book I'll share with friends and read again. Catch ya later—I'm headed for the woods."

KIX BROOKS, country music artist, Brooks & Dunn

"To look at nature with wonder and awe is to marvel at its glow. To see nature with knowledge and detail is to understand its truth. To view it through Rob Simbeck's eyes, the reader gets to embrace everything good about the beauty of nature in every possible way."

HOLLY GLEASON, editor of *Woman Walk the Line: How the Women in Country Music Changed Our Lives*

"Some of my earliest memories are of the outdoors and it's a place where I still find peace today. Rob Simbeck's stories of everything from the cottontail to the hummingbird bring me back home to Tennessee no matter where I find myself in the world."

CRAIG MORGAN, country music artist

"Rob Simbeck is the consummate storyteller—informative, engaging, enlightening. *The Southern Wildlife Watcher* offers a superb blend of outdoor education and entertainment. Simbeck's stories of familiar and less well-known inhabitants of the natural world will appeal to all who appreciate the outdoors, even those who stay indoors."

WHIT GIBBONS, professor emeritus of ecology, University of Georgia

"With the publication of this incredible collection of wildlife stories, Rob Simbeck takes his place in the company of truly great nature writers such as Hal Borland, Donald Culross Peattie, Herbert Ravenel Sass, and John Burroughs. His creature biographies reveal fascinating facts about animals that will stir readers to leave their armchairs and go outdoors to observe firsthand the denizens of woods, fields, oceans, and streams. Simbeck possesses a naturalist's keen awareness of mother nature's harsh realities but also has a sympathetic eye for the details that make her charming. The result is one of those rare books destined to be read again and again, each time with fresh enjoyment."

KEITH "CATFISH" SUTTON, author of *Hardcore Catfishing*

The Southern Wildlife Watcher

The Southern Wildlife Watcher

Notes of a Naturalist

Rob Simbeck

FOREWORD BY JIM CASADA

THE UNIVERSITY OF
SOUTH CAROLINA PRESS

© 2020 University of South Carolina

Published by the University of South Carolina Press
Columbia, South Carolina 29208

www.uscpress.com

Manufactured in the United States of America

29 28 27 26 25 24 23 22 21 20
10 9 8 7 6 5 4 3 2 1

Library of Congress Cataloging-in-Publication Data
can be found at http://catalog.loc.gov/.

ISBN: 978-1-64336-092-8 (paperback)
ISBN: 978-1-64336-093-5 (ebook)

To Linda Renshaw

and to all those who work for the benefit of the natural world

Contents

Land

PART II.

Water

PART III.

Foreword

All creatures, great and small, have always intrigued me. As a youngster I spent endless happy hours in carefree pursuits involving insects: touching roly-polies (pill bugs) to watch them curl into a tight ball; catching June bugs and tying them to strings and then flying my insect helicopter until the hapless, tethered captive tired of the whole affair; chasing lightning bugs in the gloaming; tempting ant lions by using a broom sedge stalk to fool them into thinking wayward prey had blundered into their conical sand traps; or raiding the hearth and home of yellow jackets, wasps, or hornets in a quest for fishing bait. The fact that the latter endeavor involved a delicious bit of danger merely made it more enticing.

Then there were my larks as a lepidopterist, with a fishing net serving me well in capturing species of butterflies such as monarchs, skippers, black and tiger swallowtails, and painted ladies. These fragile, lovely creatures paid the ultimate price by becoming bedroom adornments carefully pinned to large pieces of cardboard. Occasionally there would be a particularly special moment such as when I obtained a zebra swallowtail or found a fragile, lovely luna moth in all its lime-green glory. Looking back, I realize this all sounds rather brutal, but I grew up "country," as part and parcel of my youth, and such behavior was the norm.

It wasn't just insects that tempted me like forbidden fruit. Birds and mammals enthralled me in a variety of ways—the interesting, informative, and sometimes comical behavior of birds, especially during the spring mating season, found me watching nests in wonder, taking peeks at clutches of eggs, or listening enchanted to symphonies of song. As a hunter, I learned woodsmanship and all its many attributes—patience, stealth, the ability to keep still, how to read sign, and much more—as a top-line predator.

When weather, attendance in school, parental restrictions, or other considerations kept me from actually interacting with nature in a direct fashion, I did so vicariously. By the time I was midway through high school I had read and in many cases reread every volume in the local public library that in any way dealt with natural history, exploration, hunting, fishing, or related subjects. American authors such as Roy Chapman Andrews, Henry David Thoreau, Henry Van Dyke, Theodore Roosevelt, and Aldo Leopold became trusted guides, amply buttressed in charting my literary path by British counterparts such as Charles Darwin, Thomas Bewick, and especially Gilbert White. The great African explorers—Dr. David Livingstone, Henry Morton Stanley, John Hanning Speke, Verney Lovett Cameron, Harry H. Johnson, and Frederick C. Selous—also fascinated me because they combined discovery with hunting and in-depth field work as natural historians.

All these youthful "yearnings and yonderings," as my paternal grandfather sometimes described them, came tumbling back to me in a sumptuous mélange of memory when I first encountered Rob Simbeck's "For Wildlife Watchers" column in the pages of *South Carolina Wildlife*. This was well before I knew the man, who has since become a cherished friend, but I immediately recognized a kindred spirit and an exceptionally skilled wordsmith. In issue after issue of the magazine, his tight, bright little essays served as sparkling reminders of the truth inherent in words provided by a leading sporting scribe from yesteryear, Horace Kephart: "In the school of the outdoors there is no graduation day."

Simbeck may not even recognize the name Kephart, who was once known as the "Dean of American Campers," but his columns leave no doubt whatsoever that curiosity is a close, constant companion of those who love the world of the wilds. Over time, as I read columns that were as delightfully diverse in their subject matter as they were consistently well informed and appealing, it dawned on me that skilled writing, backed by careful research, could turn the seemingly mundane to magic. For example, who would think that visits to the world of the common house fly or the red velvet ant could be fascinating? What sort of misguided mindset would select moles and earthworms as subjects? Does fascination with great white sharks and copperheads suggest preoccupation with creatures perilous to man?

I'll leave it to individual readers to draw their own conclusions about Simbeck's choice of subject matter, but here you have a full three-dozen examples of wildlife, grouped in three simple categories according to their habitat—air, land, or water—that serve as sterling reminders that our world in general, and that of the Southeast in particular, is one where there's wildlife of interest at every turn. My Grandpa Joe, while he lacked much in the way of formal education, was a superb self-trained naturalist. Little escaped his observation, and nothing that lived in his world lay outside the bounds of his curiosity. He and Rob Simbeck would have been kindred spirits.

This is not a book that highlights majestic wild game animals such as white-tailed deer and wild turkeys. The two game animals covered are the commonplace eastern cottontail and the gray squirrel. Nor does it emphasize the mighty or majestic at the expense of the mundane. Bald eagles and blue jays, manatees and crayfish, crows and coyotes get equal billing. You'll learn about creatures that may well be new, such as the whitetail dragonfly or the wolf spider, while the likes of ruby-throated hummingbirds and pileated woodpeckers, both of which are pretty much unforgettable, may seem old friends.

Whatever the critter in question, though, I can virtually guarantee that, unless you are a highly trained specialist, you will learn something new. That's partly thanks to the easygoing, immensely readable approach the author takes to his subjects, but it's also the result of his turning to experts for the type of insight only an authority would be able to offer. That's something few of our great nature writers—such as John James Audubon, John Burroughs, John K. Terres, and Archibald Rutledge (just to show that being named John is not a prerequisite)—have done. The approach adds depth, credibility, and authenticity, and, when blended with masterful prose, it's a fine formula for producing a book that merits a prominent place on the shelves of anyone interested in the world around us.

This is the type of book that lends itself to back-porch or bedside reading. Each chapter in effect stands alone, a compact little jewel with facets such as unusual characteristics, feeding and breeding behavior, the place of the species in the grander scheme of nature's ways, life cycles, preferred habitat, and the keys to existence for each species covered. Whether read an essay at a time or from beginning to end in a single sitting (it's captivating enough to invite such an approach), this is a special book. As someone whose life has gained treasure beyond measure through close interaction with and observation of the natural world, I know it will hold a place of pride in that section of my library devoted to conveying awareness of the creatures that share a world we sometimes wrongly describe as "ours." When you have turned the last page of this most welcome anthology, I predict you will have precisely the same reaction as that expressed by the literary critic Walter Besant after he read works by the great English natural historian Richard Jeffries, including *The Story of My Heart, The Amateur Poacher, Round about a Great Estate,* and *Wild Life in a Southern County:* "Why, we must have been blind most of our lives; here were the most wonderful things possible going on under our very noses, but we saw them not."

Rob Simbeck exposes those things "going on under our very noses," not in the English countryside but in the southeastern United States. In doing so he makes a singular contribution to the rich trove of writing on the region's natural history.

JIM CASADA

Preface

This book is a love story, a record of my appreciation for the creatures around us—large and small, drab and flashy. These essays sing the praises of the fox and the frog, the shark and the spider, the owl and the oyster.

I am someone for whom a walk in the woods is an adventure—and a trip home. I am a fan of St. Francis and the Japanese haiku master Issa, both of whom felt to their marrow our kinship with every other species. It is a kinship writ in DNA against the backdrop of a world we share all too briefly. The same molecules that drive our ability to design computers help the crow to fly, the snake to crawl, and the fish to swim.

This is also a love story in the sense that the woman I have shared my life with for more than thirty years is the one who opened my eyes to the world as I see it. Debby gave me the gift of nature, helping me build a relationship with it that combines casual intimacy and deep reverence, one walk in the woods, across a field, or along the beach at a time. In every piece collected here, I have hoped to catch a bit of the sacred ordinary in all its guises, placing the quotidian details of each species' reality inside a frame of wonder.

The readers of *South Carolina Wildlife* have shared this journey with me since 1994. The stories herein appeared first, sometimes in different form, in the magazine. We have explored the outdoors together, conversing as if by the fireplace in a cabin, in relaxed appreciation of all we've seen—"emotion recollected in tranquility," as Wordsworth termed the genesis of poetry. We are simply expanding the conversation here, inviting in lovers of the outdoors from Virginia to Texas, from Arkansas to Florida, hoping to find among their number people who carry a poet's soul as a complement to good hiking shoes and binoculars.

Within our appreciation for nature and its creatures lie the seeds of responsibility. If we are not moved by what we observe, if those creatures do not speak to us, we might as well be dead already. There is always a bigger picture, and it lies with us as never before to assess the impact we have on the world and its inhabitants and to choose the world we will bequeath to our progeny.

I hope to share within these pages the magic I feel when I encounter the natural world, for we are all part of a cosmic Ferris wheel, whirling around together on this pretty blue planet. May this book unite us in that appreciation, and may it connect us more fully to the creatures around us.

Air

PART I

American Crow

It all started when we got chickens. As I'd work in my study at the back of the house, I found I could tell what was going on with them just by listening to the amount and tenor of the cackling. Eventually I knew the birth notices ("Hey! I just laid an egg!") from the more agitated Neighborhood Watch ("Hey! The Kellys' cat is out again!"). The ultimate in over-the-top pandemonium was reserved for the approach of a red fox, which was greeted with the clamor you'd expect from a prison riot or perhaps the explosion of a circus calliope.

I'd keep an ear half-cocked as I worked, and that led me to pick up on the doings of wild birds as well. I could hear the ordinary, peaceful goings-on, as songs and contact calls erupted here and there on the lawn or in the nearby woods. Mockingbirds sang, titmice fussed, and robins cheeped.

It wasn't long before I knew when there was a real crisis, which, of course, I'd always use as an excuse to spring from my chair and into the yard. It was then that I learned to appreciate the family Corvidae, since probably

75 percent of the real action around here involves its principal eastern ambassadors, blue jays and crows, which *The Audubon Society Encyclopedia of North American Birds* calls "some of the most bold, active, noisy, and aggressive of all birds." Believe it.

A lot of cawing generally means the crows are in posse mode, usually in reaction to an owl or hawk in the neighborhood. In fact, I've probably seen more owls by responding to the complaints of crows than by any other means. Hawks and owls, especially great horned owls, are crow predators, eating both adults and young, and crows—I don't blame them for this—will simply not abide their daytime presence. They will gather around such an intruder, harassing it with a barrage of mobile noise and driving it off.

Nature being what it is, though, crows have no trouble being the aggressors. The other major form of noise involves some smaller species screamingly trying to drive off a crow. Any observant birder can frequently spot mockingbirds, blue jays, or other species dive-bombing and harassing fleeing crows. One spring I heard the shrill cheeping alarms of robins in the tree just outside my window. I looked out just in time to see a crow carry off a nestling.

Crows will eat pretty much anything, from grain and insects to roadkill and human corpses. Their appearance on the battlefields and cemeteries of centuries past helped give crows and their close relatives the ravens a decidedly morbid reputation.

"But," says John J. Marzluff, professor of forest sciences at the University of Washington, "they have also stimulated our art, language, and religious beliefs. Native Americans from California to southeast Alaska worshipped raven as a trickster and creator. According to their beliefs, raven brought the moon, stars, and sun to the world and peopled it as well. Even today, as one walks the streets of Juneau, Alaska, you can meet people of the raven clan. Japanese artists of the Edo period regularly created great screens featuring gatherings of crows, birds that symbolized to them strong social bonds. More English words today are derived from the words 'crow' and 'raven' than from any other wild animal. Remember that when you use a *crowbar,* examine your *crowsfeet,* or feel *ravenous.*"

Their penchant for grain has long earned crows the enmity of farmers (think scarecrows), and some states had bounties on their heads for years. Their chief survival tactic in that regard has been their remarkable intelligence. A number of experiments, in labs and in nature, indicate that crows can count. Send three hunters into a blind to shoot at them, and they'll keep their distance. Send three in and two back out, and the crows still won't come near. It's not until you send five or more in and all but one back out that you can fool them.

Their brains, as you might suspect, are larger in relation to their bodies than those of just about any other bird. "This large brain," says Marzluff, "packed tightly with the same type of nerve cells that comprise our own brains, works much as does ours." The advantage of that intelligence manifests itself in many ways. They have excellent memories when it comes to hiding and re-finding food. Crows post guards when they filch grain. They have been seen pulling up ice fishermen's lines to eat what's on the hook. Scientists have found twenty-three distinct forms of calls, and crows are terrific mimics.

"Crows recognize particular humans and remember their past offerings or transgressions for years," adds Marzluff. "On the University of Washington campus, crows treat researchers that have captured them just as they treat owls. For over thirteen years now, these local birds remember and attack researchers when they don the mask initially worn to catch a few birds. Today, most of the birds so engaged learned about the masked person by hearsay—they were not even born when the captures occurred! This ability to recognize, remember, and pass on information depends on the crow's remarkable brain and its efficient social lifestyle, which ought to sound pretty familiar."

Crows are monogamous and mate for life. Their courtship is elaborate, with the male bringing food to his mate and engaging in taxing flights, fancy bowing, and dancing. Both sexes spend about twelve days building the nest, which is a big basket of sticks and twigs two feet across, lined with grass, moss, fur, and leaves. As the naval term "crow's nest" suggests, they are generally placed very high in trees. The female lays four to six splotched, grayish-green eggs and incubates them by herself for eighteen days while the male feeds her. Both parents care for the young, which can fly at about a month old.

During the breeding season, crows are territorial but will make allowances when necessary.

"In some settings, where new territory is hard to come by," says Marzluff, "young males may remain with their parents for several years as 'helpers.' They watch for intruders and predators and even feed their siblings as they bide their time until breeding space opens up." In the fall and winter, they may gather in remarkable numbers. I have seen them in flocks of several thousand, descending on a group of trees to roost for the night, and they have been known to assemble in much larger roosts. One, in Fort Cobb,

Oklahoma, noted in a count published in 1972, was estimated to contain two million birds. And, yes, a gathering like that is called a murder of crows.

The American crow is related closely to the fish crow, which looks like a slightly smaller and thinner copy and differs in call and diet, and to the raven, which is twice as large and inhabits more montane locations. Over most of the Southeast, when you're away from the coast or a waterway, you're more than likely looking at an American crow. The fish crow is coastal throughout the Southeast from the Carolinas south and is found in all of Florida. It can also be found in major river systems and up the Mississippi Valley to Illinois and Indiana.

If you're unsure, the call is your ticket. The American crow is known for that bold "caw, caw," while the fish crow's is a much more tentative and nasal "wah, wah," sounding more like a timid quack.

There is nothing timid, of course, about the call or the behavior of the American crow, whose loud, aggressive nature makes it clear that colorful birds can come quite plainly in basic black.

American Crow

DESCRIPTION: 18–20 inches in length, wingspan 36 inches; iridescent black, with thick bill and short, rounded tail.

RANGE AND HABITAT: Throughout North America; throughout the Southeast, in almost any habitat.

VIEWING TIPS: Smart and adaptable, they're likely to be found most anywhere in the region. Listen for that raspy caw. This is one where you just keep an eye and an ear out.

Monarch Butterfly

To become a dedicated wildlife watcher is to lose yourself to wonder. It is to marvel at the bud and the blossom, the goldfinch's molt and the spider's web. It is to treasure the cicada's buzz, the frog's croak, and the groundhog's waddle, to relish the dolphin's breach, the bumblebee's flight, and the blue jay's wheedling call.

Even amid all that, there are phenomena that stand out, that become ever more dumbfounding the closer we look and the more we ponder. Take the monarch butterfly. In its journey, its annual resurgence, its sheer unbidden beauty, we find an encapsulation of all that is transporting about the natural world.

Four inches from wing tip to wing tip, a monarch weighs half as much as a dollar bill and has a brain the size of a peppercorn. And yet every fall, millions of them, just a few weeks old, begin an epic migration. From Canada and much of the United States east of the Rockies they head south over terrain they have never seen, toward a dozen specks of forest—most part of the Monarch Butterfly Biosphere Reserve—in the mountains of southern Mexico, a gathering place not known to scientists until 1975. There, in fir trees nearly two miles above sea level, they congregate to ride out the winter in a display that led the entomologist Lincoln Brower, known for his research into and work toward protection of the monarch, to write: "I couldn't believe the density and numbers. . . . It was like walking into Chartres Cathedral and seeing light coming through stained-glass windows. This was the eighth wonder of the world."

They rely on stored fat until, with the coming of spring, they mate and head north, beginning an incredible cycle yet again. Meanwhile, monarchs west of the Rockies generally overwinter in Monterey pines and cypresses along the California coast.

Scientists are still learning how the process works, how after three generations of butterflies that live for a month or six weeks, one—the Methuselah generation—can live for more than half a year, dodging predators, replenishing its reserves with nectar drawn through a half-inch-long tube called a proboscis, then gathering in a place cold enough to slow their metabolism but warm enough to keep them from freezing to death.

Few people know monarchs or their behavior as well as Billy McCord of the South Carolina Department of Natural Resources. He has studied them for decades, personally tagging more than forty thousand, and he has witnessed aspects of that overland journey few others have.

"Based on tag recovery data," he says, "we know they can move as much as a hundred miles a day when conditions are ideal, soaring on thermals. I used to help with studies of the fall migration of birds of prey, and you'd see monarchs a thousand feet up or higher, the same plane where raptors were migrating."

As magnificent as the facts of that journey are, scientists and wildlife watchers alike know that the migration and the North American population of monarchs (there are monarchs in other parts of the world) are in trouble. Logging has had an effect on the extent of their winter grounds, although that has been addressed in recent years. A much bigger problem appears to be herbicide-resistant corn and soybeans, which allow for the more extensive use of herbicides and the subsequent killing of more species, among them the milkweed family, the monarch's sole host plants. More than 160 million acres of milkweed habitat have been lost in recent years to herbicides and development, according to University of Kansas figures.

The monarch's numbers were once almost unimaginable—an estimated 300 million of them overwintered in Mexico, closely packed together and covering more than fifty acres total. A single storm in 2002 killed an estimated 75 to 80 percent of them—a quarter of a billion monarchs. By 2015, there were just 42 million covering three acres. In 2016 and 2017, the numbers were 150 million and 100 million, respectively. Meanwhile, the overwintering California population stands at fewer than thirty thousand butterflies, down from more than four million in the 1980s.

In the Southeast, we see monarchs most often during spring and fall migration.

"They are uncommon as a summer breeding species throughout the Southeast," says McCord. "The vast majority of migratory monarchs are produced in the northern tier of the U.S. and southern Canada." In the spring, they have historically taken advantage of the more than forty species of milkweed and their relatives found in the longleaf pine ecosystem that was once much more common in the region, but their numbers have dwindled here as well—a 2018 survey reported in the *Journal of Natural History* found that the population in northcentral Florida had declined by 80 percent since 2005. McCord's work has uncovered one of the real surprises in the study of monarchs—a wintering population in his home state of South Carolina, one of a handful of such populations reported in the Southeast, most in Florida and Texas.

While those west of the Appalachians fly on to Mexico, McCord says those east of the mountain chain, and particularly those migrating south near the Atlantic coast, don't seem to do that, with many of those that arrive along the South Carolina coast through early November continuing to move south to south Florida. There, he says, "they continue to burn sugar they get through nectar, and the prevailing wisdom is that they just become absorbed into local nonmigratory populations, their primary focus to find a member of the opposite sex and reproduce. Such insects will not live through winter or migrate back north the following spring."

Those that arrive in South Carolina in mid-November or later are more likely to spend the winter along a thin coastal zone, surviving, like their counterparts in Mexico, California, and a handful of other spots in the Southeast, on stored body fat and brief feeding forays during occasional winter warm-ups.

"I have caught nearly three thousand individual monarchs at least once after I made the original capture, one of them on seventeen different days at Patriots Point, Mt. Pleasant, between Christmas Eve and early March," says McCord. He caught another at Folly Beach on November 12, 2011, and caught it a second time on March 9, 2012, 117 days after he tagged it. "So, I have a lot of data showing that some do at least attempt to pass the winter along the immediate coast in central Charleston County. My suspicion is that such wintering behavior may occur in a region very near the coast of much of the South Carolina coastal region, with the majority along the central part. It's potentially a little too cold north of Winyah Bay, and if you get to the Georgia coast it may be too mild. Within this region, the climatic conditions on the coastal islands and on the mainland adjacent to salt marsh or to the ocean can be almost identical to high-altitude Mexico, with average temperatures in the forties at night and fifties during the day from December to late February and into March."

The zone in question is the immediate coast, "not farther than half a mile from the saltwater or salt marsh because of the moderating effect of the water on the temperature. The Carolinas don't produce many breeding populations of monarchs. That's what is so potentially important. There's nothing approaching the populations in Mexico, but it was quite a shock to me to find breeding populations."

It is a find that represents a new wrinkle in an already impressive and increasingly fragile natural history.

Monarchs from throughout North America and others found in pockets around the world share a common life cycle. A female lays hundreds of pin-head-sized eggs on the leaves or stems of milkweed plants, generally one or perhaps a few per leaf. In about four days, each becomes a squirming cater-pillar that chews a hole in its egg case and emerges. It eats the egg case, then begins devouring leaves, growing and molting four times until it reaches two inches in length. Those milkweed leaves, by the way, contain glycoside chemicals that make the caterpillar—and the butterfly it will become—poisonous to most birds, and the butterfly's bright colors are thought to telegraph that danger.

After several weeks, the caterpillar undergoes a fifth molt. It spins a silken pad onto a leaf or twig, hangs itself up by a hook-like appendage at the end of its abdomen, splits its skin, and wriggles out as a chrysalis that undergoes one of nature's most remarkable transformations. Though it looks like a lime green, gold-spotted part of a plant, it is for the next ten days a cauldron of chemical activity. Enzymes dissolve its tissues, but what looks like a soupy mess contains organized groups of cells called imaginal discs that develop into each part of the adult body. Finally, the chrysalis becomes transpar-ent, the orange and black of the wings showing through. Then, on the next weather friendly day, one of nature's most gorgeous creatures emerges, dries itself in the morning sun, and flies off.

The monarch, like all insects, is composed of a head, thorax, and abdo-men. It has six legs, four wings, and enormous compound eyes made up of thousands of light-sensing ommatidia. It is also covered with tiny receptors called sensilla, located on its proboscis, antennae, palps, legs, feet, and wing bases, that allow it to gather tastes and smells essentially all over its body. Veins carry a copper-based, bloodlike substance called hemolymph, which is blue green rather than red and contains proteins and sugars rather than oxygen. Adults dine on nectar from many kinds of plants, pollinating some as they go.

In central North America, overwintering monarchs again head north in the spring. For the millions in Mexico, that may mean laying eggs on the first available milkweed species in northern Mexico, Texas, or nearby states. From there, the next generation continues toward the northern reaches of the continent's milkweed plants.

"Those that first head north," says McCord, "are four to six months old and have spent the last several months in trees. They are weathered, worn, and weakened, and they put their last energy into reproduction, using milk-weed plants in northern Mexico or along the Texas gulf coast."

But they produce a next generation that continues the journey, which ends as far north as southern Canada and disperses monarchs across the country. The fact that the migration is in jeopardy is the kind of crisis that makes it incumbent upon all of us to reflect and, wherever possible, act on the plight of the continent's monarchs even as we appreciate the rugged stained-glass beauty of those that grace our own region.

Monarch Butterfly

DESCRIPTION: Beautiful orange-black butterfly with white spots on wing margins; 3½- to 4-inch wingspan. Slight difference in sexes. Sometimes confused with the smaller viceroy.

RANGE AND HABITAT: Fields, meadows, gardens, roadsides throughout North America—wherever you find milkweed. Some populations in the Caribbean, Australia, Europe. Winters in Mexico, California, and along a tight strip of South Carolina coast and a few other southern locations.

VIEWING TIPS: Warm weather. Caterpillars dine exclusively on milkweeds and closely related plants. Adults gather nectar from variety of flowers and occasionally take liquid from the ground.

Ruby-Throated Hummingbird

"Sit here on the porch," Debby said one Sunday afternoon in early summer. "I want to show you my hummingbirds." We had just started dating, and I had come to visit her at her little white house in the country.

She picked up something that looked like an hourglass with several tiny red saxophones sticking out the bottom. I soon learned it was a humming-bird feeder, but my knowledge of flora, fauna, and their associated hardware was so rudimentary at the time that I had no idea.

She walked a few paces into the yard and stood holding the gadget about a foot in front of her face, which wore a look of determined expectation. She stood this way for several minutes, her arm crooked at a 45-degree angle, until I began to believe the hummingbirds might be imaginary and that I should think about tiptoeing toward my car.

Soon, though, something that sounded like a tiny atomic cat purring zipped across my field of vision. It stopped a few feet from her and the feeder, hanging in midair like a battery-operated Christmas ornament, its body angled kind of like the Concorde. It eyed her, eyed the feeder, and moved in for a drink. Debby lit up like she'd just been named Miss America, and I have to admit I was pretty impressed too. The thing had a black throat—or at least it looked black until the sun caught it just right, when it glowed like bright red coals. Its back was a nearly-as-pretty iridescent green. It was feeding inches from Debby's face.

Soon it was joined by another, this one with a white throat, which moved in for its own drink. They buzzed back and forth, drinking for a bit, zipping off to the edge of the woods, then coming back, for about ten minutes, until Debby's arm finally gave out. She came back to me and smiled. "Pretty good, huh?" she said. It was. It really was.

She called them Dipper and Zippy, and they became part of Birding 101, which I took concurrently with Debby 101. After a while I learned to love all three of them, and she and I and the hummingbirds' descendants—along with the occasional dog, cat, horse, and chickens—have lived in and around that little white house in the country ever since, and I write about all of them now and then.

Hummingbirds were great to learn about, primarily because there's only one species that nests east of the Mississippi. "That," I could tell summer visitors with the breezy assurance of a tour guide at the Smithsonian, "is the ruby-throated hummingbird." With sparrows or warblers, on the other hand, I had to keep quiet, because there were scads of them and they all looked alike to me.

Much of their natural history seemed to be written in superlatives. They're the smallest birds—the ruby-throated is a little over three inches long, and the Cuban bee hummingbird is an inch shorter. Their wings, three to four inches across, beat more than seventy times a second when they're flying forward, a little slower when they're hovering or backing up. They can also, by the way, fly straight up and down. The wingbeats indicate just how high these birds are revved—hummingbirds have the highest metabolic rate of any animal, with the possible exception of the shrew. That being the case, they need to eat pretty much all their waking hours. Their tiny crops enable them to store food overnight, and they sometimes enter a dormant state called torpor, reducing their metabolic rate by up to 70 percent to endure cold weather.

Though a hummingbird brain is smaller than a pea, it is larger relative to the bird's size than that of any other bird. Studies suggest a hummingbird knows the flowers in its territory and when each will fill with nectar, the main component of its diet and something it draws from flowers (or feeders) with a tongue that extrudes, often several times a second, from a very slightly downcurved bill. Among the many hummingbird friendly native plants in and around our yard are cardinal flower and trumpet creeper, both red and both hummingbird magnets. The "red" part of that equation, though, points to a widely accepted notion about hummingbirds that doesn't really hold up under scrutiny.

"It's not that hummingbirds are particularly attracted to red," says Dr. Bill Hilton Jr., executive director of Hilton Pond Center for Piedmont Natural History, near York, South Carolina. "Many experiments have shown they're attracted to almost anything novel and will return if there's nectar involved. My thinking is that red is the most easily seen color against the green of nature. Not coincidentally, many tubular flowers are easy-to-see red in color and have high nectar loads that attract hummers." Hummingbirds, in fact, have cones in their retinas that seem to be more sensitive to red and yellow, although it's been shown that nectar is a better draw than color. And whether or not a feeder is red, the nectar itself shouldn't be, as the red dye is unnecessary and possibly harmful.

Hummingbirds carry an almost magical air with many people, and the fact that so many of us are using feeders and plants to draw them in is among the reasons the hummer's population is strong throughout the Southeast.

Male ruby-throats—the ones with the red gorgets—are fiercely protective of their territories and will attack and drive off other hummingbirds, bumblebees, hawk moths, and even kingbirds and crows. Hilton once watched as a hummingbird appeared to drive off a red-tailed hawk. "The gram-to-gram ratio there is pretty significant, when you think about it," he says. The male will swing back and forth like he's on the end of a pendulum, making a series of quick, high-pitched cheeps before rushing at an intruder. We've seen and heard two male hummingbirds fly right into each other.

Hummingbirds satisfy their need for protein with bugs, ants, flies, and spiders, which they can generally find in abundance on flowers. We have also watched them pick bugs out of spider webs, an activity that, given their size, can be fraught with peril—they have been known to become entangled in the webs. Their size also leaves them vulnerable to other unexpected dangers. Frogs have snatched them out of the air, and birds, including shrikes, kestrels, and hawks, have been known to take them.

Their size does guarantee relative safety for ruby-throated nests, at least from human interference, since they're almost impossible to find. The size of a golf ball, a hummingbird nest is made solely by the female from ferns, weeds, leaves, and thistles and held together with silk from spiders or tent caterpillars. Then, it's covered with bits of lichen and moss until it looks just like any other lichen-covered lump on a branch. She lays two pea-sized eggs and incubates them for about two weeks. The hatchlings are as voracious as any baby birds and, says Hilton, "Female ruby-throated hummingbirds carry a slurry of nectar and tiny invertebrates in their crops, and regurgitate this nutritious food into the gaping mouths of their young."

They will stay in the nest for two to three weeks, depending on temperature and the availability of food, and near the end of that period, says Hilton, "the chicks are so large the female must perch nearby." She may continue to feed them for at least several days after they fledge.

Mating and nesting follow the absolute wonder that is hummingbird migration. I don't know about where you live, but there's a lot of excitement here about when the hummingbirds will arrive each spring. Keeping up with who's got their feeders out and who's seen them is a big part of it. Generally, it happens by the end of February or the first week of March along the Gulf from Texas to Florida, with April 1 a pretty good benchmark along I-40 and mid-April for the upper regions of the Southeast. It may be mid-May until those at the far reach of their range, in northern Canada, arrive at their nesting grounds. Males arrive first and establish territories, then mate with one or more females, using elaborate displays and dives in their courtship.

That arrival marks the return from a trip that started the previous fall, when some of these tiny creatures, weighing just one-seventh of an ounce, traveled overland to Mexico or Central America. Others, eating until they nearly doubled their weight, meanwhile trekked five hundred miles over the open water of the Gulf of Mexico. It could be the most impressive and memorable thing I know about hummingbirds.

Except for the fact that I once watched two of them eat from a feeder a country girl held out in front of her thirty years ago and fell in love with all three.

Ruby-Throated Hummingbird

DESCRIPTION: 3-inch-long, gray-white underside, emerald green on back and crown; adult male has ruby-red throat; immature resembles female but sometimes with dark throat streaking and one or more red feathers.
RANGE AND HABITAT: Summers and breeds in eastern U.S. and southern Canada as far as west as eastern British Columbia. Throughout the Southeast except extreme southern Florida. Winters in southern Florida, southern Mexico, and Central America as far as western Panama.
VIEWING TIPS: Birds of the edge (not open or heavily wooded habitats). Frequent visitors to favorite flowers. Will come to feeders.

House Fly

Don't kill that fly!
　　Look! He wrings his hands,
　　　　He wrings his feet!

Leave it to Issa, the St. Francis of Japan's haiku masters, to remind us that it's possible to empathize even with a house fly, if we will just pause for a close-up.

We may see them as vermin, but Issa bids us to reconsider. Is his little fly fretting? Praying? Let us, as wildlife watchers, give Issa his due and reconsider as well. Actually, wonder of wonders, the fly is bathing, much as a cat would. It rubs its legs over its head, thorax, wings, and abdomen, scrubbing its eyes, its antennae, and the bristles on its legs and body, then rubs those legs together and against its mouth to brush away grime. It's vital work, since flies, like vultures, spend a lot of time around filth, and since each body part is essential for finding food and drink and avoiding predators, each is worth dedicated maintenance.

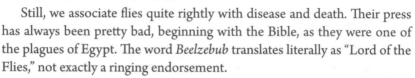

Still, we associate flies quite rightly with disease and death. Their press has always been pretty bad, beginning with the Bible, as they were one of the plagues of Egypt. The word *Beelzebub* translates literally as "Lord of the Flies," not exactly a ringing endorsement.

It's worth noting that North America was once without them. The house fly—one of 150,000 species of flies so far described—is actually an Asian native that has followed humans around the globe, as we and the animals we domesticate produce two things flies love, namely garbage and feces, both great nutritional sources for them and their offspring.

Two characteristics of flies make this a bad deal for us humans. First, to use the high-dollar words, flies regurgitate and defecate on pretty much everything. The former softens and liquefies food so it can be drawn in through a sponge-like proboscis. The latter is, in this case, a distressingly frequent activity. Second, they're microbe magnets and have been known to carry more than a hundred pathogens, including anthrax, typhoid, dysentery, cholera, and E. coli. In fact, a single fly can carry more than a million microbes. Think about that when one of them moves from a dog dropping to your salad. Amazingly, they seem to be immune to all of them.

None of this would be of much consequence if they reproduced at the rate of, say, pandas or polar bears, but short-lived creatures tend to make sport while they may. Flies are ready to mate quite young—twenty-four hours after emerging as an adult for females and as few as sixteen for males.

"Being slightly smaller, males may develop slightly quicker than females in the same conditions," says Eric Benson, an extension entomologist and professor emeritus of entomology at Clemson University. "Females only mate once, and it behooves the males to be ready and able to mate before the females fully develop so they can get the girl of their dreams."

Females lay from 75 to 150 white eggs, in a location offering moisture and nutrition, several times over three or four days, laying five hundred to six hundred eggs altogether. Just about one thirty-second of an inch long, an egg can hatch in eight to ten hours in very warm weather into a smooth white maggot, which begins eating and grows to two-fifths of an inch in three to seven days, looking ultimately like a wriggling grain of white rice.

The maggots shed their skin several times, then crawl to somewhere cool, dark, and dry. There, they turn into pupae, their hard, brown shells offering protection. In three days to three weeks, they develop legs, wings, and all the rest in a process as fascinating and mysterious as that of the butterfly, whatever we think of them aesthetically. The adult breaks through the case and emerges full-size, about a quarter of an inch long. The entire cycle, from egg to adult, can take as little as a week, with three weeks being the average.

The house fly's head swivels on a small neck and is dominated by two reddish eyes, each with four thousand six-sided lenses working independently and providing wide-angle vision that gives it a great advantage in fleeing predators—as do the hairs all over its body.

"House flies are very good fliers," says Benson, "but they are covered in an exoskeleton, which is like flying in a suit of armor. The hairs help them process and evaluate information in their environment. Many probably detect air currents, direction, and speed. Hairs on the antennae detect odors for food. Hairs on their tarsi (feet) function as 'taste buds.' This is why flies often walk around in circles when they land on food."

The fly's body is divided into thorax and abdomen, the former gray with four longitudinal stripes and home to the wings and legs, the latter yellowish with a dark median line. Its veined, transparent wings can beat two hundred times per second in a figure-eight pattern, and 11 percent of its total body mass is dedicated to the muscles that drive them. It can fly at five miles per hour and travel a couple of miles, if necessary, to find food and water. Most insects have four wings, but house flies are from the order Diptera, meaning "two winged." The other pair gradually evolved into knobbed filaments that aid in stability.

A fly's six segmented feet have curved claws and wet, sticky hairs that allow them to cling to pretty much anything—horizontal, vertical, or upside-down. A 1945 study sought to learn how they landed on ceilings, and slow-motion film showed they used a half roll rather than an inside loop. To disengage, they twist and pull each foot free.

Everything is pretty simple here—a fly's brain is essentially a big nerve mass called a cerebral ganglion, the digestive system a long, busy tube, the circulatory system an open heart that sloshes blood around, the respiratory system a number of tracheal tubes branching from pores called spiracles—but it's enough to do the trick.

Given their reproductive rate, if all of the descendants of a single pair lived, they would cover the earth to the height of two and a half feet in just a few months. "This makes house flies a very important food resource for many animals," says Benson. Spiders, beetles, mites, birds, frogs, and other reptiles eat them, as do parasitic wasps that burrow into the shells of the pupae. Most never really get going; less-than-ideal conditions—too wet, too cold—often inhibit or stop development of eggs, larvae, and pupae.

While cockroaches, termites, ants, and bedbugs are "probably more important pests for the average pest control company than house flies," Benson says, "fly control in restaurants and food prep areas is extremely important and ongoing. Flies in general, and house flies specifically, can get out of control quickly, so, compared to other pests, house flies can become the most important pest in a structure literally overnight."

It doesn't take many house flies to repopulate an area if conditions are right. And so, while we may not get to Issa's level of empathy, as wildlife watchers it may behoove us to cast a more appreciative eye their way when we, as we inevitably must, interact with them.

House Fly

DESCRIPTION: About one-fourth of an inch long; gray thorax with stripes; yellowish abdomen with median stripe.

RANGE AND HABITAT: One of the world's most widely distributed insects.

VIEWING TIPS: They'll find you. They're especially attracted to manure, food scraps, and anything dead.

Eastern Screech Owl

There is, in the waning light of dusk, an interlude where time suspends itself. In summer, the many shades of green that have colored the day give way to a single hue, charcoal gray. Fireflies rise lazily, blinking like languid champagne bubbles. Crickets, tree frogs, and bullfrogs begin their evening symphony. In winter, naked branches release the last strands of light to chilled air, and the planets and stars take their cold, bright places. It is time for laying aside the burdens of thought as surely as we hang the rakes or axes in their places. The chores that aren't yet done will wait until morning.

I will always think of dusk as the Cardinal Hour, when the feeder birds have all settled onto perches for the night, except for the cardinals, no longer splashes of brilliant red but rather crested silhouettes lingering in the last fleeting moments before the night shift.

Given the highly uncertain nature of life on the wing, however, dusk is not always so kind to the cardinals themselves. Screech owls, it turns out, are big fans of the Cardinal Hour, but for far more utilitarian reasons. Those lingering cardinals are moving about just as the owls begin a night of predation. That makes them, according to Lex Glover, former wildlife technician with the Wildlife Diversity Programs of the South Carolina Department of Natural Resources, "perfect screech owl food."

Glover has studied and banded screech owls, and he has poked through enough owl pellets—the regurgitated undigestibles they throw up after meals swallowed whole—and looked over enough nests to get a good feel for their diets. "Cardinals are out after other birds have roosted," he says. "They're vulnerable at that time, and I've probably found more cardinal feathers in screech owl nests than any other kind."

Of course, there is plenty more on the screech owl menu.

"They have one of the most varied diets of any owl species," adds Andrew Arnold, director of education and outreach at the Alabama Wildlife Center in Pelham, Alabama. "Cardinals are a common prey item, especially in suburban areas, but so are house sparrows, starlings, finches, blue jays, and so many other birds. And, of course, there is the huge variety of non-bird food items like small mammals and snakes and more aquatic items like frogs and salamanders for those living near water. Plus, the quantity of soft-bodied insects such as worms they eat is likely underestimated, since they can fully digest them and thus they wouldn't show up in their pellets the way fur and bones do."

Whether it's eating birds or mammals, insects or amphibians, the screech owl, despite its diminutive size (on average, just an inch or so longer than the cardinal), is a formidable predator. It has excellent hearing, with offset ears that let it pinpoint sound, and big yellow eyes designed for night vision. It will drop from a branch and, thanks to the construction of its wings and feathers, take to the air in silence. In full flight, it can detect the movement and direction of mice and voles under a layer of leaves and snatch one up, even in the dark. Its winter diet contains more mammals, which may reach the size of flying squirrels, while in spring and summer it leans toward grasshoppers, frogs, moths, beetles, small bats, and birds.

Owls have long impressed people. Their stealth and nocturnal presence once suggested supernatural powers, an idea that continues to make them one symbol of Halloween. There is a superstition that hearing an owl call means death and disaster are near. It doesn't hurt that the screech owl's call is a real attention-getter on an otherwise still and moonless night, sounding somewhat like a horse's whinny, occasionally mixed with a soft hoot.

The owl's reputation for wisdom likely came from its appearance—big eyes and ponderous head movements suggesting great powers of observation and, perhaps, deliberation. The head movements and eye size are actually two sides of the same coin. To facilitate night vision, the owl's eyes evolved to such a size that they fill space that might otherwise be occupied by muscles to move them, necessitating the head turning, which can extend to 270 degrees, thanks to fourteen cervical vertebrae, as compared to a human's 180 degrees and seven cervical vertebrae.

At eight to ten inches in length, the screech owl is a little shorter, top to bottom, than a robin, but its wingspan, at twenty-two inches, is several inches longer; males are up to 15 percent smaller than females. The screech owl looks like a miniature version of a great horned owl, which also has big yellow eyes and feather tufts that look like erect ears or horns. Its coloration—there are rufous, brown, and gray color phases—helps keep it inconspicuous, and the bird can heighten the effect by narrowing its eyes to slits and erecting its tufts so that it more closely resembles a branch stump.

The screech owl is itself prey to snakes, skunks, hawks, larger owls, and sometimes even other screech owls, and its eggs are vulnerable to snakes and raccoons, among others. Crows and jays that run across it during the day will often mob it, with smaller birds joining in. When threatened, screech owls may snap their bills, making a sharp popping sound. They can, in turn, be very aggressive when nesting, diving at intruders, including people, that get too close. They nest in tree cavities, such as abandoned woodpecker holes, in nesting ranges from ten to seventy-five acres. Home ranges can reach two hundred acres and are much less vigorously defended, often overlapping with those of other screech owls.

"They are very common and can be found almost anywhere in the Southeast," says Arnold, "as long as there is adequate woodland. They really like being close to water sources as well. They even do very well in suburban areas, mostly because they will use manmade nest boxes if natural cavities are not available and because suburban areas have fewer predators for them to worry about."

Mating occurs in late winter. The female lays three to six nearly round, white eggs, which she incubates for twenty-six days, with the male often bringing food. Both parents feed the young, making up to seventy trips a night, until they leave the nest after about a month. At first, they are still weak and inexperienced flyers but are terrific climbers, using their feet and beaks to move around in trees.

"Their zygodactyl feet are a cool adaptation," says Arnold. "They can shift one of their toes so they have two on each side, which is extremely useful for helping young owls to climb before they are fully flighted."

As their skills improve, they begin hunting with their parents, and, late in the summer or early fall, they will move to their own territories, often nearby.

The screech owl's numbers are, according to Glover, steady, a fact that helps keep some destructive mammals, particularly rodents, in check. Despite its occasional predilection for cardinals and other favored backyard birds, the screech owl is definitely a welcome addition to our nighttime skies.

Eastern Screech Owl

DESCRIPTION: 8–10 inches in length, 22-inch wingspan. Ear tufts, yellow eyes. Looks like a miniature great horned owl. Brown, gray, and rufous color phases.

RANGE AND HABITAT: Deciduous or mixed forests near fields; wooded parks, suburbs, throughout eastern U.S.

VIEWING TIPS: Much easier to hear than see. Trilling note, and an unnerving whinnying screech.

Common Whitetail Dragonfly

In nature, fact often trumps fiction. Take dragonflies, for instance. Many people in the South refer to these quick, clear-winged insects as "snake doctors" for their reputed ability to stitch up wounded snakes with thread stolen from spider webs. Mothers looking for a way to up the ante on the old wash-your-mouth-out-with-soap ploy sometimes maintain that if you cuss, a dragonfly just might sneak up on you and sew your lips together.

It's perfectly serviceable fiction, since it's not hard to imagine the long, slender abdomens of some dragonfly species doing needlework.

The facts are even better. Dragonfly nymphs capture and eat prey bigger than themselves. They will chow down on mosquito-sized fish, tadpoles, even baby snakes. The nymphs can also propel themselves with a primitive form of jet propulsion by—there may be no way to phrase this delicately—blowing gas out of their rears. The adult's two pairs of wings, clear with large black patches in the middle, move independently, so it can work them in opposite directions and hover in one spot, then switch them to unison and zip off forward or backward. The dragonfly has "wraparound" eyes that cover most of its head and give it nearly 360-degree peripheral vision. Then, to top it off, there is reproduction.

Just a few days into their adult lives, males stake out and defend territory, often in spots along ponds, streams, lakes, or bays containing good sites for females to lay eggs, perching on a plant or on the ground when not engaged in defending territory or mating.

From his post, a male will rush out, grab, and mate with a passing female. He curls the tip of his abdomen and deposits a sperm packet in a chamber in his own abdomen. Then he grips the female by the head or neck with grasping appendages called cerci at the rear of his abdomen and induces her to bend her abdomen to pick up the packet. While the exchange is going on, the two are in a position called a mating wheel, which is unique among insects and often formed in the air.

She then extends her abdomen as she hovers over the water and, sometimes with the male still attached, sometimes with him hovering nearby and keeping other males away, touches the surface to wash off up to four dozen eggs in anything from a good-sized pond to a small puddle.

"The common whitetail is a real generalist," says Richard Connors, a naturalist, wildlife photographer, and biologist retired from the Tennessee State Parks system. "Some dragonflies have very specific habitat needs, including pristine water, but whitetails can use most any kind of water, including degraded habitat with low oxygenation. A whitetail will be happy to occupy a nice mud puddle if it's going to be there long enough that the eggs can hatch and emerge. Not all dragonflies are that adaptable."

The process of mating and protecting the female has been known to take its toll.

"The male may literally wear himself out during the process," Connors says. "You can tell by looking at the wings—if they're tattered and dirty, he's probably been battling a lot and then guarding that next generation of eggs as the female lays them."

The eggs may incubate for as little as five to ten days, or for as long as several months, in the case of those that overwinter, depending on conditions. In either case, they hatch into nymphs that feed on tiny crustaceans and protozoa. There may be eight to fifteen molts over the course of several months to two years, depending on the species. The whitetail nymph grows to be about an inch long, with large eyes, six legs and small wing buds extending from its thorax, and a large oval abdomen with gills at the opening to its rectum, which is why it's able to force air out for that bit of jet propulsion.

The grown nymph is quite the hunter, waiting motionless underwater until detecting prey. The next step is quick and deadly, thanks to a lower jaw that resembles a folded backhoe, complete with pincers at the tip.

"That lip shoots out," says Connors, "and captures prey that can be as large as the nymph itself. They're voracious predators." Their order name, Odonata, in fact derives from the Latin root for "tooth," referring to that lower jaw.

The dragonfly will go directly from this form to adulthood.

"Theirs is an incomplete metamorphosis," says Connors. "There is no chrysalis formed as a middle stage, as there is with butterflies. In this case, a fully-grown naiad crawls out of the water." As it does so, the skin on its thorax splits, releasing the adult, which also has two forms—a pre-reproductive phase lasting a few days and a sexually mature phase lasting a few weeks.

"You'll see the females and males, looking very much alike except for slightly different patterns on the wings, in a meadow or on a hilltop or at the side of a country lane, away from the water before they mature," says Connors, "feeding on mosquitoes and other insects," including butterflies and moths. Then it's on to the process of reproduction.

There are about 500 species of dragonflies and damselflies in the United States and Canada and 250 or so in the Southeast, where they are widespread and common. The whitetail can be seen beginning in March along the Gulf Coast, a little later farther north.

"They're a sign of spring," says Connors. "They can emerge from shallow habitats that warm quickly, and it's always a joy to see them then, maybe sitting on a warm rock out of the wind. They can go through more than one generation in a year, and in the fall they can survive a frost and can be seen sometimes until the first hard freeze."

The common whitetail is present in all forty-eight contiguous states. The species gets its name from the adult male's bold, white abdomen, which it holds in such a way as to show it off while perching. That white coloration is actually a powdery substance called pruinose that covers the abdomen like a coat of chalk dust. The female's abdomen, on the other hand, is brown with a row of yellow spots. Both have shiny brown heads, gray/brown thoraxes with yellow or white striping, and narrow, transparent wings with two or three broad, dark bands.

Fossils indicate that dragonflies have been around for a third of a billion years, since well before the dinosaurs. They have earned major places in folklore around the world, with names like "horse stinger" and "devil's darning needle." The larger species can inflict a harmless bite, but these are insects that pose no worries to humans. In fact, they are actually very beneficial predators, destroying huge numbers of mosquitoes.

In the larval stages, whitetails are prey to fishes, birds, and other larvae, as well as larger dragonflies. When they first emerge as adults, they are prey to birds, but once they gain flight experience, their agility keeps them fairly well protected, although they are susceptible to mites and other parasites.

These are highly visible insects, and it's not hard to understand Connors's fascination with them. Their reputation for needlepoint may be wrongheaded, but they have definitely sewn up a spot among nature's most impressive creatures.

Common Whitetail Dragonfly

DESCRIPTION: 2 inches long with conspicuous white tail on adult male. Spends most of life as a nymph with an extrudable lower jaw that makes it a formidable predator.

RANGE AND HABITAT: Widespread and common throughout Southeast.

VIEWING TIPS: March through October, near fresh water.

Pileated Woodpecker

Some people think of them as the crown jewels of birding, but warblers have never excited me much. Sure, they're pretty, but much of warbler watching consists of straining for peeks at little birds that flit and flutter in the tree-tops, then thumbing through a field guide trying to tell them apart.

I'm a woodpecker guy. Give me something with a mating bongo you can hear for half a mile and a call that's a loud and raucous variation of Curly's (of Three Stooges fame) "Nyuk, nyuk." I want a bird as big as a crow with a fiery spurt of red on its harlequin head, showing great splashes of white under its wings as it flies from tree to tree. I am speaking, of course, of the pileated woodpecker, which sits atop my personal list of favorite birds.

The pileated will work a tree with a rocking, spring-loaded motion, in earnest pursuit of the carpenter ants and wood-boring beetles that make up the bulk of its diet. It chisels at the bark, then goes after the insects with a tongue that is several inches long (it wraps around its skull) and is tipped with barbs and coated with sticky saliva. The bird's hearing is so acute it can actually hear its little snacks moving about.

It has other features that are no less impressive. That red-crested head is one big shock absorber—the skull is strong and thick, and there is a thin space between the brain and a tough membrane lining. Its neck muscles are powerful enough for the aforementioned bark-stripping, its nostrils are covered with feathers to keep out flying wood chips, and its tail feathers form a sturdy brace to help cushion the body from all that pounding.

Now, if all this makes the pileated sound like the swaggering, yo-ho-ho-ing, one-eyed pirate of the bird world, it's worth explaining that this is a bird that knows when to play it coy. The pileated is wary of people, and it generally seems to be on the opposite side of a tree from us. Stealth is a good tool for pileated watchers.

Aboriginal America was very much to the liking of the pileated. It prefers mature wooded areas—deciduous, coniferous, or mixed—with good numbers of dead, standing trees. Swampy areas are particularly attractive.

American Indians often used pileated feathers to adorn their calumets, or peace pipes, and the birds were killed for food as well as for adornment. Their numbers began to decline seriously with the advance of European

settlers, who cleared forests and shot the birds for sport or food. By the end of the nineteenth century, pileateds were rare throughout the eastern United States, but gradually secondary forest growth brought their numbers back. Their range currently extends from the South's bottomlands and swamps through the mixed evergreen/deciduous forests of the northeast, across southern Canada to the Pacific Northwest. They are fairly common in well-wooded areas of the Southeast, and in fact their numbers in much of the region have increased rather dramatically over the past fifty years.

Where you've got them, it is the pileated's calls that will often alert you to its whereabouts. Its wucka-wucka-wucka resembles that of the flicker but is louder and more resonant. A slower, sharp, and irregular kek-kek is used in keeping contact between partners and with young; a wik-wik-wik call is used in mating and in expressing territorial dominance. The pileated's drumming is also proportionally louder and more resonant than that of its smaller cousins, and under good conditions it can be heard for nearly a mile.

A nest may be in a live pine or soft deciduous tree, but most often it is from fifteen to seventy-five feet up in a dead, limbless, barkless stub. Males and females both excavate cavities, with the male doing the bulk of the work, sometimes starting several before choosing one to complete over the course of three to six weeks. The only lining consists of leftover wood chips. The oblong hole generally faces east or south, probably to catch the sun's early morning rays, and it leads to a one- to two-foot deep, cone-shaped chamber both sexes guard fervently.

The female lays from three to five white oblong eggs and incubates them for 15–18 days. The hatchlings are featherless and helpless, and for the first week to ten days, the parents go completely inside the nest to feed them. Then the young are tall enough that the parents, with the female feeding more often than the male, can lean in while clutching the tree. By two weeks of age, the young wait at the entrance for their returning parents. They fledge at 24–28 days old and remain near the nest for several days.

A number of other birds and mammals benefit from the pileated's tendency to excavate more holes than it needs. Flying squirrels, wood ducks, screech owls, bluebirds, various swallows, American kestrels, great-crested flycatchers, and others have all taken over pileated holes. Several species also benefit from the pileated's presence by following them onto trees they've stripped and eating the insects they've uncovered.

Pileateds have only a few enemies. They'll give a Cooper's or sharp-shinned hawk a good run for it, dodging through heavy woods. Peregrine falcons have an easier time and take them from the air.

Generally, though, it is the destruction of forests that poses the greatest threat to pileated woodpeckers. For now, their numbers remain strong in most of the Southeast, and it's still relatively easy, with a little knowledge and stealth, to enjoy this red-thatched wonder.

Pileated Woodpecker

DESCRIPTION: 16–19 inches long; 24- to 30-inch wingspan; black with red crest and white down the side of the throat and on the wings. Undulating flight.

Luna Moth

Most animals, like most people, aren't fated to win beauty pageants. The world is teeming with creatures that don't hold up well under aesthetically driven scrutiny. Among insects, for instance, it's not easy to find support for Keats's dictum that truth is beauty and vice versa. Truth with a magnifying glass fares even worse. There are nearly a million species of beetles, clearly making them a triumph of survival and adaptation, but they are not near the top of the list of creatures adorning greeting cards.

Butterflies are, of course, the big exception. Light, ephemeral, dazzlingly colored, they capture our minds and emotions, helping to give insects what little cachet they have. With moths, on the other hand, it would seem we are flapping back into the realm of the average, the pale, and the ordinary.

But that, according to Rita Venable, former editor of *Butterfly Gardener* for the North American Butterfly Association and author of *Butterflies of Tennessee*, is not the case. She points to the new *Peterson Field Guide to Moths of Southeastern North America*, which celebrates what it calls "the incredible diversity found in the world of moths."

Perhaps nowhere is the beauty within that diversity more evident than in the luna moth. Coming across one provides one of nature's loveliest surprises. "Their long tails," says Venable, "trail and toss behind their large wings. They look like miniature lime-green kites flying around. You can't help but stop and watch one when you see it."

They hold many attractions. They are, first of all, large, up to six inches in length, with a wingspan that can exceed four inches. They are strikingly beautiful, their vibrant lime green color sometimes edged with maroon or yellow highlights and transparent eyespots on each of four wings. But, as they are nocturnal and spend only a brief time in the adult stage, we are likely to miss them, fairylike, as they mate and reproduce, passing their genes to the next generation. The adult luna moth has not even been granted a mouth by evolution, so it lives off fat ingested in the last days of its caterpillar stage, as it mates, then weakens and starves to death in a week or so.

The luna moth is named for Luna, Roman goddess of the moon. It is a member of the giant silkworm family, one not related to the Oriental silk-producing moths. It prefers deciduous hardwood forests and occurs from Canada to Florida along the East Coast and west to Nebraska, Kansas, Oklahoma, and Texas.

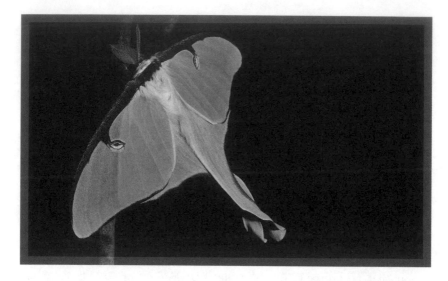

"It is not an uncommon species in the Southeast," says Billy McCord, a wildlife biologist with the Marine Resources Division of the South Carolina Department of Natural Resources. "There are enough rural areas and swamp forests with plenty of sweetgum, hickory, pecan, and other larval host plants that the species is still doing well."

Procreation takes place during that very brief adult phase, which begins with a midmorning emergence from the cocoon. The female is already full of eggs, holding from 150 to 250, and several hours after nightfall she emits a pheromone from a gland at the back of her abdomen. Males, who can sense the pheromone from a great distance with feathery antennae, find the females, and the two mate, remaining joined for hours. The female begins laying eggs, a few at a time, on the underside of food plant leaves. The effort burns the fat she has stored, and she is dead not long after. The male is more than likely able to fertilize several females, but he will not live long either. Latitude affects the number of broods, which varies from one in the north to three along the Gulf Coast.

Adults can be seen in every month in Louisiana and Florida. Moving north, the first overwintering cocoons emerge as adults in March or early

April. Weather conditions, particularly rainfall, help determine the timing of the second brood, which can vary from late May through early July. A third brood can emerge from August 1 to mid-September, and even a partial fourth is possible.

The eggs hatch in about ten days into caterpillars that are eating machines. They grow through five larval stages, spending about a week in each, with the fifth lasting a little longer, the skin splitting each time as they grow. The caterpillar is thick and green with a brown head, a yellow stripe down each side, and rows of red tubercles. It gets to be three and a half inches long before entering the pupal stage, spinning silk from near its mouth and wrapping itself in a cocoon, often with a leaf as an additional layer. In many cases it drops to the ground before doing so, wrapping itself with whatever is available and becoming virtually impossible to spot amid the leaf litter. That makes it important, according to Venable, that people "leave the leaves" in their yards.

Normally, it is in the pupal state for two to three weeks, except for those that overwinter. Emergence begins with the secretion of a liquid that helps soften the cocoon, which the moth scrapes and tears with small spikes at the end of its forewings. It squeezes through a small hole and crawls onto a tree trunk or branch.

There are conflicting reports on the overall health of luna moth populations.

"I don't think there's any doubt that localized populations have suffered greatly from urban sprawl, increased numbers of electric lights [which disrupt mating and navigation], pesticide use, and loss of larval food plants," says McCord, "but over the broad scope of things, the southeastern population is probably still in pretty good condition."

Natural predators include parasitic wasps, spiders, toads, birds, including owls, and bats, which face a challenge with the luna moth. A 2015 study in the *Proceedings of the National Academy of Sciences* suggests that a luna moth's tails flap in such a way as to throw off a bat's echolocation, increasing its chance of survival.

Luna moths have no equivalent natural deflection for the perils humankind throws up at them, so Venable has some useful suggestions: "Don't capture, leave the leaves, take photos and share, educate others, don't use pesticides, plant hostplant trees, encourage public officials to use native trees in landscaping, and limit your use of electrical lighting at night."

As for seeing them, it's possible for a dedicated wildlife watcher to do so during the day.

"Scan the vegetation near their hostplant trees," says Venable. In addition to those already cited, those include birch, cherry, hickory, beech, walnut, persimmon, and sumac. "There, they may be seen mating, drying their wings, or just resting and very still during the daytime."

Day or night, they are sure to delight any wildlife watcher. If we do our part, we can help preserve suitable habitat for the luna moth and give ourselves continued opportunity to cross paths with one of nature's loveliest and most ethereal creatures.

Luna Moth

DESCRIPTION: 3- to 4-inch wingspan. White body; pinkish legs; lime green wings with eyespots; feathery antennae.
HABITAT AND RANGE: Deciduous hardwood forests along the East Coast from Canada to Florida. Across the Southeast.
VIEWING TIPS: Brief breeding periods, especially in spring, offer the most predictable opportunities. Rural areas, particularly near woods with water.

American Robin

For naturalist Roger Tory Peterson, it was an encounter with a flicker that "made me aware of the world in which we live." For South Carolina Department of Natural Resources wildlife technician Lex Glover, who has made a life out of his love for the natural world, it was a much more common bird.

"I was in high school," he says, "and we had robin nest just outside the kitchen window in a dogwood tree. I'd sit at the window and watch them, and I remember the parents coming to the nest with mouthfuls of earthworms and just shoving them down the babies' throats. I thought they were such excellent parents—after feeding them they would just perch at the edge of the nest and watch the young and look around. It was a neat experience, and I was bummed that I wasn't there when they fledged. I credit that with helping to get me into birding."

The sheer ubiquity of robins has no doubt inspired many other young people to pay more attention to nature. In fact, as a little boy, I thought the word "bird" referred exclusively to the orange-breasted creature that seemed as much a part of our lawn as the grass. The robin was by far the most common bird where I grew up in Pennsylvania, and it didn't seem possible to scan the yard without seeing its distinctive hop, that cocked-headed once-over of the ground, and the earnest tug that meant an unlucky worm was now a meal. Its sturdy nest often sat where I could see it, in one of the bushes at the front of the house or on a low branch of a black cherry or other hardwood. Its song, variations on a musical *cheerily, cheer up,* was the signature sound of dawn and dusk.

The robin is among the most abundant birds on the continent, with a population estimated at more than 300 million. It lives in almost every habitat, from forest to tundra, from Central America to north of the Arctic Circle, from sea level to twelve thousand feet. It is, of course, quite at home in human landscapes including yards and parks.

People have noticed. "When the Red, Red Robin (Comes Bob, Bob, Bobbin' Along)" was a hit several times between the 1920s and 1950s, and "Rockin' Robin," "Fly, Robin, Fly," Joan Baez's "Diamonds and Rust," and Randy Travis's "Deeper Than the Holler" all name-check it. It has appeared in Emily Dickinson poetry, in Native American mythology, and on a Canadian $2 bill. The robin is the state bird of Connecticut, Michigan, and Wisconsin; since 1993 its egg's well-known shade has been a Crayola crayon color.

Early American colonists named it after its smaller, orange-breasted European namesake. The American robin is a thrush, part of a group of songbirds that includes bluebirds, the veery, and hermit and wood thrushes, which often possess attractive plumage and spotted breasts, particularly in the young. The robin is the largest of the American thrushes, at ten inches long, with a wingspan of fourteen to sixteen inches and an average weight of two and a half to three ounces. That orange breast sets off a black head and tail with white around the eyes, a yellow bill, black-and-white-streaked throat, grayish brown back, and white under the tail. Male colors are bolder than those of the female, and, true to form, juveniles have spotted breasts.

Worms are an obvious favorite in the spring and summer, but caterpillars, grasshoppers, other insects, and their grubs form a large part of their diet as well. In the fall and winter, robins eat much more fruit, with chokecherries, juniper berries, hawthorn, and dogwood among their favorites.

With autumn comes a southward migration, although some robins can be found wintering in even hostile climates, eating the berries remaining in wooded, densely vegetated areas. With fall and winter, according to Glover, the species' population swells in the Southeast, as robins move in from northern states and Canada, sometimes on their way to Florida and the Gulf States.

"These winter flocks move around a fair bit as they look for food," says Glover. "When we do Christmas counts, you can often see large numbers of robins either first thing in the morning or the last thing in the evening, often going into bottomland hardwood areas where there is plenty of cover, and maybe cedars and evergreens so they have a place to roost. I have also seen them in plowed fields, with sparrows and blackbirds mixed in with them."

Robins are among the first birds to return to northern breeding grounds in the spring, and so they are one of the season's iconic symbols. They begin courtship soon after their return. Males, which generally arrive a week or two before females, sing to attract them, then raise and spread their tails, shake their wings, and inflate their throats. Pairs sometimes approach each other with their bills open and touch them together. Males also sing to establish nesting territories, and both sexes defend breeding territories.

The female chooses the nest site, usually from five to fifteen feet off the ground. Robins have been known to nest in eaves, gutters, or other parts of buildings as well as in trees and shrubs. The nest, built by the female, is six to eight inches in diameter, strong and circular, reinforced with mud, with a soft inner lining of grass. She will lay from three to five light-blue eggs and incubate them for about two weeks. Their early nesting, says Glover, means they are susceptible to spring storms, which can damage or destroy the nest or subject the eggs or young to fatal chilling if the mother must leave to feed.

The young are featherless, and their eyes remain closed for the first few days. As Glover can attest, both parents bring worms, berries, and insects many times a day. Crows and blue jays will take young from nests, and eggs and young are also susceptible to squirrels, snakes, and other predators. Robins raise "cheep!" alarm calls and fly at perceived threats. Studies show that only about 40 percent of nests are successful and that just a quarter of young robins reach a year of age. The young leave the nest in two weeks but stay close and beg food from parents, who accommodate them for a time. In another two weeks they are able to sustain flight. Robins typically raise a second brood.

Cats, larger snakes such as the rat snake, and hawks, falcons, and owls all prey on adult robins. They are susceptible to parasitic worms and are known to be carriers of West Nile virus. Still, this is one species that is thriving in close quarters with humans. It is an intimate, sharing the spring morning and the summer evening with us.

Wildlife watchers often thrive on sightings of the rare and unusual, but experience teaches us an ever-renewed appreciation for the ordinary. For those of us in the United States, the American robin is quintessentially ordinary, but its quirky presence can serve as a quotidian delight, a constant reminder of the riches to be found all around us.

American Robin

DESCRIPTION: About 10 inches long; gray back; black head; bold orange breast.
RANGE AND HABITAT: Varied; Alaska to Central America. Nests throughout Southeast.
VIEWING TIPS: Familiar call. Often spotted in yards. One of the easiest birds to see and hear.

Carpenter Bee

Humans have been good for a lot of species. We're not talking here about the ones we've domesticated, because for most of them the arrangement has been a decidedly mixed blessing. But there are birds, including robins and mockingbirds, that are a lot more numerous since we've changed the North

American landscape. Starlings have a whole new continent to inhabit thanks to us. Rats and mice are doing awfully well, too, attracted to our stockpiles and leftovers.

Then there are the insects drawn to our homes and outbuildings, such as paper and potter wasps, mud daubers, and termites. This is a generally unwelcome group we spend a good deal of time and energy trying to keep at bay.

When it comes to one such visitor, the carpenter bee, you will not find Whit Gibbons among that group.

"I say, 'Just enjoy them,'" says Gibbons, professor emeritus of ecology at the University of Georgia's Savannah River Ecology Laboratory in Aiken and an outdoor author. "I have them on my back porch, and every spring I'm sitting there and little shavings are falling on what I'm reading or in my hair."

Now, the sight of insects that are dead ringers for bumblebees hanging around the deck or porch and, for good measure, drilling holes into eaves and ceilings might seem like a solid counterargument, but Gibbons shoos it away.

"I don't tell anybody to try control them, and I definitely wouldn't say to use pesticides on them. They won't be around long in any given year, and they've been drilling holes in our deck for at least ten years and the deck's still here. Meanwhile, they've given us a lot of enjoyment."

It's part of a nature friendly outlook that has made life a lot more interesting for his kids and grandchildren.

"Anything you find outside can be exciting," he says. "It's a continual learning experience. We know where every log and rock in the back yard is because we're always turning them over. I've got three grandsons who would rather get outside and look for animals than play video games."

Of course, it doesn't hurt that, thanks to his work, Gibbons can bring home the occasional baby alligator, but the point is a great one. More of us need to enjoy the nature that's closest to us, and, to hear him tell it, the lowly carpenter bee can be as entertaining as just about anything.

"I'll get the kids and grandkids and say, 'Everyone put on a yellow hat or shirt,' and the bees will come after us—they respond to yellow. The males are so territorial they'll try to run off anything that comes near. Last year we watched a particular male who hovered above a little bush every day, from daylight 'til dusk. You'd walk over and he'd come toward you."

That's not as risky as it might sound. Since stingers are modified ovipositors, male carpenter bees don't have them. Females do, but they're normally at work, too busy to bother with humans—and unlikely to do so unless actually handled.

Telling them apart is simple enough—males have a patch of white on their faces, while females' faces are black. Telling them from bumblebees starts with where they are. Bumblebees have underground nests and so are usually close to the ground. If there's one around the eaves or over your head, it's probably a carpenter bee. The main physical difference is that the abdomen of the bumblebee is fuzzy and yellow, while the carpenter bee's is glossy, black, and hairless.

The holes the females excavate are for nesting. Using their tough mandibles, they will chew nearly round holes three-eighths of an inch in diameter into soft and preferably unpainted wood, then turn right after an inch or two and chew a tunnel four to six inches in length at the rate of six days per inch. She creates brood cells along the length of the tunnel, forming a ball of pollen and regurgitated nectar, laying an egg on top and walling it off with a bit of chewed wood pulp—she does not eat the wood.

The egg, proportionally one of the largest in the insect world—she may lay only a dozen or so—has all the nourishment it needs to grow from grub-like larva to pupa to adult in about seven weeks, by which time the female has died. The fully formed adults chew through the cell partitions and crawl, over each other if necessary, to emerge in late August. They gather and store pollen in the same corridor, living and overwintering there.

They emerge again in April or May, when the process begins again. Once male and female mate, the female gathers nectar and excavates, and the male stations himself where he can decide whether to mate with or chase off whatever comes his way. Humans are just one more large intruder to be dealt with and, as Gibbons points out, once you know they're harmless, it can be fun to have them get up close and personal.

Females will clean out old tunnels to reuse and extend them several feet. They will also dig several corridors from the same vertical shaft. The excavation rarely if ever causes enough damage to harm the structure, although woodpeckers will sometimes dig through the wood for grubs or adults.

There are five hundred species of carpenter bees worldwide, but the primary one in the Southeast is the eastern carpenter bee, which can be found widely east of the Rockies. The other one sometimes spotted here is the southern carpenter bee, which is much smaller and nests in trees—which is also what carpenter bees do when our dwellings aren't handy.

Carpenter bees are excellent pollinators when it comes to open-faced flowers, and so they're useful for many fruits, including pears, peaches, apples, plums, and blackberries. On flowers with deep corollas, though, they'll often use those strong mandibles to tear into the side of the corolla, swiping nectar without picking up or depositing pollen. Blueberry growers are consequently no more fond of them than some homeowners.

Gibbons would like to see the number of fans—or at least interested observers—of the species increase, and given their utility as pollinators, their harmless natures, and the fact that they do not in fact cause meaningful damage to homes, it may not be a bad bandwagon to join.

Carpenter Bee

DESCRIPTION: Like a bumblebee with a hairless abdomen.

RANGE AND HABITAT: New England to Florida, west to Texas and Nebraska. Throughout Southeast.

VIEWING TIPS: Most of us don't seek them out, but if you've got them, enjoy the show!

Bald Eagle

Let's start with Ben Franklin, who floated the idea of the turkey as our national symbol rather than the striking raptor that got the nod. Not everyone, after all, is familiar with his reasoning, tongue in cheek though it may have been. In January 1784, he wrote: "I wish the bald eagle had not been chosen as the representative of our country; he is a bird of bad moral character; he does not get his living honestly; you may have seen him perched on some dead tree, where, too lazy to fish for himself, he watches the labor of the fishing-hawk [osprey]; and when that diligent bird has at length taken a fish, and is bearing it to his nest for the support of his mate and the young ones, the bald eagle pursues him and takes it from him. . . . For in truth, the turkey is in comparison a much more respectable bird."

I'll have to admit the eagle is not the hardest-working bird I've ever seen. I've not seen one steal a fish, but I've watched them spend much of their time perched, seemingly just keeping an eye out for an easy meal. Bald eagles are fishers, snatching their prey—healthy, sick or dead—from the surface after a long, shallow dive or simply scavenging on the shores of lakes or rivers.

But leave it to Warren Douglas, a ranger with Reelfoot Lake State Park in northwest Tennessee and someone with a lifetime of familiarity with the region's eagles, to put it in proper perspective.

"One word that describes bald eagles is *smart*," he says. "Unlike what Ben said, they are *opportunistic* feeders and will go for the easy meal because they can, to spend less energy, which allows them to survive during inclement weather or harsh conditions."

It has been a more-than-useful tool as bald eagles continue to come back from one of the iconic population collapses and rebounds in the history of conservation. The fact that Debby and I had a weekend place on the Cumberland River below Cheatham Dam in northcentral Tennessee in the '80s and '90s gave us a ringside seat for one aspect of that comeback.

From November to March each winter, we had first one, then two, wintering eagles, probably from the Great Lakes, often in a tree not fifty yards downriver. This was at a time when, says Douglas, "we had about the only eagles in the Lower 48 here in Tennessee during the winter." By the time we sold the place, in 2000, we had a nesting pair.

Tennessee, like the rest of the Lower 48, had seen its population of bald eagles crash beginning in the 1950s, primarily because of the effects of the pesticide DDT. It entered creeks and streams from farm runoff, household use, and mosquito control and wound up inside the water's inhabitants. At the top of the aquatic food chain, large fish were often laced with high concentrations of it. Those high doses got passed to eagles, killing some and disrupting the reproductive cycles of others by causing eggshells to form so thinly the weight of the nesting female would break them. When combined with the fact that people often shot eagles and that eagles ate ducks killed with lead shot, the effect was catastrophic.

In 1965, there were 417 nesting pairs in the Lower 48, down from what is thought to be on the order of 100,000. The bald eagle had been a common nesting bird of the Atlantic coast after World War II, according to Tom Murphy, nongame biologist with the South Carolina Department of Natural Resources, but numbers reached a low point in the state in 1977, when there were just thirteen pairs left in South Carolina. There had been fourteen known nests at Reelfoot Lake in 1955. Six years later, there were none. The number was still zero when I moved to Tennessee in 1982. Florida was for a time a last refuge for them.

But in 1980, the Tennessee Wildlife Resources Agency began coordinating efforts to restore the state's eagle population, introducing fledgling eagles at various spots around the state in hopes they would one day nest there. The first successful eagle nest was constructed near Dover, Tennessee, in 1983. We bought our place on the river, about an hour from Dover, four years later.

They have been coming back ever since, with more than 1,500 nesting pairs in Florida alone, and another thousand throughout the rest of the Southeast. In South Carolina, they can often be found below the dams associated with Midlands and Upstate hydroelectric facilities. According to Murphy, it is thought that nesting there is tied in with the spawning runs of shad and herring, which provide plentiful food for adults feeding nestlings.

There are similar upticks throughout the region and beyond. Nationwide, the bald eagle has been reclassified from endangered to threatened and, says Douglas, "They are now nesting in forty-nine states, the exception being Hawaii."

That makes this the best time in the better part of a century to see these striking creatures and their truly impressive nests, each an immense pile of sticks and branches and sometimes odds and ends like cornstalks, lined with grass, moss, and weeds. Such a nest can be reused for many years, getting larger each time until in some cases it actually collapses—it can weigh more than two tons. Variations in weather, fish-spawning runs, and other variables mean eagles are sitting on nests somewhere in the United States year-round.

"What I have seen here at Reelfoot over the last thirty years," says Douglas, "is most nest preparation in the Southeast begins in early to late November and continues into January. Depending on weather, it seems like they always know when to lay their eggs, from mid-January to mid-March, to be successful. This year it was warm and most were sitting on eggs by the first day of February. The hatch was around the second week of March and the fledging was all month in June."

Both adults incubate the two (sometimes three) dull-white eggs, a little larger than chicken eggs, a process that takes a bit more than a month, and both feed the hatchlings.

Young eagles are dark brown, gradually adding bits of white here and there until, at four or five years of age, they begin to attain the distinctive white head and tail feathers. Those head feathers give it its name, which is tied not to hairlessness but to the Middle English word "balled," as in pie-bald, which referred to a patch of white.

Like many other creatures, eagles are larger the farther north you go, with those in Alaska sometimes exceeding forty inches in length. Whatever its size, the eagle's distinctive and arresting call—"scream" is a better term—is one of nature's more impressive sounds. This is a case where every aspect of the bird adds luster to its comeback, which remains strong.

"We currently have thirty-eight to forty nests on the lake," says Douglas, "and if you dropped a pin in the center of Reelfoot Lake and drew a thirty-mile circle from that pin, we have an additional sixty to seventy-five nests on or around the Mississippi River and other small lakes and streams."

The concentration has given Douglas and his compatriots a new view about territoriality and competition.

"From our observations the last thirty years, it was once believed the territory of a nesting pair of bald eagles was a mile radius or more," he says. "Now, even though they are still observant and protective of their nests and the immediate area, we have four nests within a half-mile circle on Green Island alone on Reelfoot Lake. Probably the best-educated statement to make about this is that as long as the food supply is plentiful, the carrying capacity of the area in which bald eagles nest is unknown. Here, we have yet to reach it."

And still, there is a flip side, as an increased population means more eagle/automobile collisions.

"There were at least eight incidents/collisions with cars involving bald eagles in the thirty-mile circle around the lake," says Douglas. "We look for incidents like this to increase with the population increases."

As for winter, Douglas says, "There have been at least five out of the last ten years when we have had five hundred to a thousand eagles here during cold spells, but nothing consistent or longer than a few weeks. If the lakes and streams freeze up like they did in the '70s and '80s, we would have one thousand to two thousand birds here until the thaw."

Part of the draw is the ducks and geese drawn to an area like Reelfoot.

"Waterfowl, especially around waterfowl refuges where they are concentrated," adds Douglas, "are one of the main food sources for wintering bald eagles during winter. Eagles, especially juvenile bald eagles, are going to follow migrating waterfowl, so this affects their migration patterns."

It is heartening to have witnessed the dramatic turnaround of our national symbol over the course of a few decades. It stands as an example of what can be done given will and expertise.

In the meantime, I'll have more respect for the laid-back tenacity of the bald eagle, for the opportunism Ben Franklin labeled so dismissively. And I won't lose the bit of awe that comes when watching it, for even when it is simply surveying the waterway, looking for an easy meal, this is a bird whose look embodies the raptor, making it easy to see why cooler heads than Franklin's prevailed.

Bald Eagle

DESCRIPTION: Up to 3 feet long; wingspan to more than 6 feet. Dark brown; adults with white head and tail. Unmistakable and impressive.
RANGE AND HABITAT: A great success story in the Lower 48, moving from endangered to common in many areas. Through much of Southeast, primarily near water.
VIEWING TIPS: Word travels when you've got eagles. It helps to be near fresh water, where they can be found in trees, soaring, or scavenging for fish.

Blue Jay

If you like 'em loud, flashy, and maybe a little rude, the blue jay is for you. Big and unmistakable, this is the Dennis Rodman of backyard birds, usually close by when there's trouble, alternately admired and bad-mouthed by people who can't keep their eyes off him either way.

Blue jays have been known to frustrate the fire out of hunters, telegraphing their presence to squirrels, deer, and other birds with loud cries that amount to "Yo! There's a human wandering around here."

"They and squirrels bust us all the time," says outdoor writer and former Southeastern Outdoor Press Association president Gil Lackey, "and I promise deer are keyed in on it. The flip side is they will often tell on the deer when it comes into the area. Sometimes it's a deer we never would have seen or heard had we not gotten a warning. It's one of the many woodsmanship tricks that keeps us on the edge of our seats for many hours when it might get boring otherwise."

While smaller backyard birds are picking up sunflower seeds, the blue jay will grab peanuts in the shell to hammer open. When it lands at the feeder, it's in a manner that all but kicks titmice and chickadees to one side. It has been known, in fact, to come in imitating a hawk, causing the smaller birds to scatter for cover.

Or at least it can appear that way.

"They certainly do make sounds like red-shouldered hawks, especially," says Than Boves, associate professor of ecology at Arkansas State University, "but I don't think anyone really knows for sure why this is the case, and I cannot find evidence that this imitation actually gets other birds to scatter (although it may be out there somewhere). Blue jays are larger and more aggressive than most competitors, so other birds typically would scatter anyhow when they come to a feeder or to another food source. I have heard blue jays 'imitating' red-shouldered hawks in all sorts of situations, so I am not sure there is a great adaptive explanation for it."

The blue jay's own *jeer* call brings a loud, electric buzz to woods and back yard alike, and Henry David Thoreau brought a chilly poetry to his description of the "unrelenting steel-cold scream of a jay, unmelted, that never flows into a song, a sort of wintry trumpet, screaming cold; hard, tense, frozen music, like the winter sky itself."

That call, taken up by several jays, may well mean the presence of a snake, cat, hawk, or owl, and blue jays will mob such intruders mercilessly. In fact, listening for blue jays is a good way to keep on top of nearby developments in the bird world.

The blue jay has other interesting vocalizations in its repertoire, including an odd *wheedle* that sounds like a rusty pump handle and is accompanied by head-bobbing that adds even more color to an already colorful presence.

When it comes to relating to some other species, the blue jay's personality shifts from odd to menacing, from Dennis Rodman to Hannibal Lecter.

"It robs every nest it can find," said John James Audubon, "sucks the eggs like the Crow, or tears to pieces and devours the young bird." In fact, one of Audubon's more striking works is his painting of blue jays eating eggs stolen from a nest. It's all part of dining habits that are highly varied and help ensure that blue jays prosper in a variety of settings. They also eat insects, seeds, berries, and nuts; acorns and beechnuts are favorites, as were chestnuts when they were plentiful. Blue jays sometimes bury acorns and, like squirrels, are known to help reforestation and the spreading of oaks. They may supplement their diets with mice, spiders, tree frogs, salamanders, snails, and caterpillars.

In any season, if you've got blue jays nearby, you'll know it. This is a big bird—ten to twelve inches long, bigger than robins or cardinals—with unmistakable coloring and a noisy nature. It is, after all, a member of the family Corvidae, which includes crows and magpies—there's not a wallflower in the bunch. Its white face is topped with a bright blue crest and bounded by a black necklace. The blue back has black stripes and white spots, and the underside is white or grayish.

Blue jays are common in much of the Southeast, in open woodlands, parks, and suburbs, but they are not as common as they used to be.

"According to the Breeding Bird Survey, which has been conducted every year since 1966," says Boves, "the blue jay population in the southeastern United States has declined significantly in most areas, with numbers declining in some regions, such as the Southeastern Coastal Plain, by more than an estimated 1 percent a year. I know they and other corvids are susceptible to West Nile virus, so in areas where West Nile is present, they seem to have declined even more rapidly."

Mating season gets under way by early March in Florida, later farther north, with the male undertaking a courtship flight, head bobbing, and courtship feeding of the female. This period brings out what subtlety and shyness dwell within this bird, sometimes accompanied by a very low, pleasant song.

The nest is bulky, made of sticks, twigs, leaves, moss, grass, scraps of paper or cloth, and mud, generally ten feet or more off the ground on a horizontal branch or in the crotch of a tree. Construction can take from a few days to a few weeks, and, says Boves, "eggs may not be laid until several weeks after initiation of nest-building," although such delays "decrease significantly with lateness of season."

Blue jays have also been known—I don't think this is going to surprise us—to appropriate forcefully the nests of other birds, including robins. There are generally four or five inch-long eggs, olive with dark-brown spots, and there is usually a second brood. They are incubated for seventeen days, and the young fledge after seventeen to twenty-one days, although they sometimes beg food even after fledging. Blue jays will defend a nest vigorously, dive-bombing cats or people who get too near.

Large, noisy feeding groups travel together as fall approaches, sometimes joined by red-headed woodpeckers. In the winter, birds move short distances to better food sources—perhaps to hardwood forests where they can eat mast—although they are not true migrants. They also, of course, make good use of backyard feeders, and it's then that we get to take time to enjoy what is generally a great show from one of the back yard's most flamboyant visitors.

Blue Jay

DESCRIPTION: 10–12 inches long; blue above with white and black striping; white below. White face with black necklace.

RANGE AND HABITAT: Widespread, woods and wooded suburbs throughout the southern U.S.

VIEWING TIPS: Watch feeders. Listen for the loud *jeer* calls.

PART II

Land

Eastern Gray Squirrel

It's entirely possible that if it weren't for the gray squirrel, we'd all be eating foods with names like "bubble and squeak" and supporting the British royal family with our tax dollars. In fact, you could make a pretty good case that this alternately lovable and maddening rodent should be our national symbol in place of the big white-hooded raptor Ben Franklin thought of as a cowardly scavenger.

The logic here goes back to the early skirmishes of the Revolutionary War. Proving we could stand up to the world's mightiest army was not going to be easy. While much of the war was fought in classic European style, with soldiers lined up in open fields firing volleys from flintlock muskets a row at a time, the colonial army at times made great headway with sharpshooters stationed behind rocks and trees, looking to take out British officers where possible, a tactic that could render British units confused and leaderless.

The preferred weapons of the colonials, who were often farmers and fron-tiersmen, were rifles, which were slower to load but far more accurate.

And where, to get to the heart of the matter, did we get our sharpshoot-ing ability? Squirrel hunting. Long-barreled squirrel rifles, shouldered by pioneers who used them to put supper on the table or keep garden pests at bay, were key in dealing with British units.

Its case as a national symbol is strengthened by the fact that the gray squirrel is probably the most commonly seen undomesticated mammal in the East, since it is active during the day and cohabits well with people in suburbs and even urban areas. It offers what amounts to free entertainment to many who enjoy its energy and antics and who feed it in parks and back yards.

Of course, there would be drawbacks. This is, after all, a rodent, a mem-ber of the most populous but least glamorous group of mammals. Plenty of people, particularly those with gardens or bird feeders to protect, refer to squirrels as bushy-tailed tree rats. There have been entire TV documentaries devoted solely to its skills at raiding bird feeders. When the eastern seaboard was loaded with virgin forests and grays were omnipresent, colonists often made it their business to dispatch them forthwith.

Ounce for ounce, the gray squirrel may be as intelligent and resourceful an animal as there is, although, unfortunately, those qualities often manifest themselves at the expense of nearby humans. The gray squirrel has also been known to steal items ranging from candy (out of vending machines) and car keys to clothing and cameras.

"I once had a pet gray squirrel," says David Osborn, wildlife research co-ordinator for the Warnell School of Forestry and Natural Resources at the University of Georgia. "She would know immediately if I had a piece of gum or candy in my pocket and would dig it out in short order."

That odd assortment of items is probably taken by the squirrel as one of three things it needs—food, nesting materials, and items to chew on to keep its ever-growing incisors trimmed.

Food normally involves twigs and buds, a little fruit, seeds, and nuts—hickory nuts, hazelnuts, acorns—with the latter often stored via burial for winter, a habit that plays an important role in seed dispersal. Shelter nests, known as dreys, are made from sticks and leaves, with an entrance facing the tree trunk, and are used for sleeping; normally, the accommodations are for one squirrel, although it may be two on cold nights. Tree dens, made of woven sticks and lined with leaves, moss, grass, pine needles, and ferns, are used for giving birth, with tree cavity nests providing better shelter for birth or sleeping, especially in winter. The teeth-trimmers can be anything from bones, shells, and shed antlers to electric lines. Pursuing the latter sometimes leads to electrocution and headlines like "Squirrel Cuts Power to 12,000 Customers."

Squirrels have good hearing and eyesight and a great sense of smell—which is how, by the way, they find those nuts again.

"Some people believe squirrels are able to remember where they bury their acorns," says Osborn. "In reality, this likely is not true. Rather, they have an exceptional ability to locate buried acorns by scent. Some of the buried acorns they discover might be theirs, but many were buried by another squirrel."

Males have overlapping territories but do establish definite pecking orders and use urine for scent marking. Females fiercely defend their nests and, if a threat is worrisome enough, will move their young elsewhere. They communicate with body and tail movements and with a variety of calls, purrs, and chucks. Their wheezy barks when annoyed are a dead giveaway to their presence, and they will attack almost anything, including people, if the nest is threatened.

The mating process can happen twice a year, if food is adequate—in late winter and again in late summer. Several males may engage in a mating chase with a single female, and females can reach sexual maturity at four months of age when abundant mast is available. Both sexes build nests, and gestation takes six weeks. The young (normally three to five) are born hairless and helpless, weighing half an ounce. They are weaned after about two months and stay with the mother ten or twelve weeks.

"I find it interesting," says Osborn, "that the mothers will move their pups among nests to provide relief from fleas when flea numbers in a particular nest become excessive."

Anatomically, the squirrel's most compelling feature is that long, fluffy tail, which besides being a communication device is used as a balance, a blanket, a parasol, a fencing foil in territorial or mating scrapes, and even a sort of parachute. The gray has grayish-brown fur, although variations from gray to reddish are possible, and a white belly.

Squirrels are sometimes migratory. Particularly in overpopulated areas, the young and others down the pecking order can be forced to move long distances. This has led, over the years, to amazing sights, with squirrels moving en masse, eating crops and crossing rivers. In 1968 millions of them did just that in an area stretching from Georgia to Vermont.

They are at home anywhere with hardwood trees, from deep woods to suburban or urban settings with treescapes. Their numbers can of course be very impressive in residential neighborhoods. Breck Carmichael, small-game project supervisor for the South Carolina Department of Natural Resources, remembers "one lady who reported capturing in her yard and dispatching ten to fifteen nuisance squirrels per month for several months in a row."

Along with hunters, automobiles are responsible for a good percentage of squirrel fatalities. Naturally, they can fall prey to rat snakes, raccoons, hawks, owls, crows, bobcats, coyotes, and foxes, not to mention dogs and cats. They are susceptible to diseases and parasites as well. Nestling mortality is high, with those in cavities having better odds. On average, squirrels live four to six years, although there are a few reported cases of gray squirrels reaching the age of ten.

There are those who find them problematic, given their attraction to bird feeders, and it's worth taking a little extra time to find a spot away from limbs or other points of access and to experiment with baffles—we've got cone baffles that keep them off ours altogether.

But this common, hyperintelligent, and persistent creature is certainly worth our grudging respect. In fact, in most cases, it's probably best to follow the advice generally given to those who have trouble with dandelions: "Learn to love 'em."

Eastern Gray Squirrel

DESCRIPTION: 10-inch body with 8-inch tail; gray with brown above, white underside.

RANGE AND HABITAT: Eastern U.S. wooded areas, including yards, parks.

VIEWING TIPS: Commonly seen in woods and in urban and suburban environments with trees.

Wolf Spider

When it comes to mating rituals, being male is a high-wire act. In most species, the male is balanced precariously between glory and humiliation, full of concentrated energy, trying desperately to please the target female. To that end, he's strutting, spreading his feathers, throwing dirt with his antlers, bringing nesting materials, singing, croaking, or roaring, showing off his plumage, voice, size, or coat. And as any male who's been single in the past thirty years can tell you, it's no picnic.

Still, perspective is everything. Sure, we can have our egos shattered and our hopes dashed. She can snarl, claw, bellow, nip, or just plain run us off. She can have another suitor waiting in the wings to charge at us. But think of the cruelest put-down you've ever heard, a response to the worst fumbling and bumbling by a would-be beau that suitordom has ever produced. Chances are, the female didn't kill and eat him.

That's something you can't always count on if you're a wolf spider. Here, the male has to do a spider break dance impressive enough that, at the very least, he doesn't become dinner after the floor show. If he can get her to cozy up to him, so much the better.

"Each species," says William Shear, biologist emeritus at Virginia's Hampden-Sydney College, "has a characteristic set of movements the males use in courtship, usually involving leglike mouthparts called pedipalps and the first pair of legs. Often, these appendages have black spots or patches of hairs that make them look larger and more obvious. Some species also have sound-producing scrapers between the joints of the pedipalps and transmit vibrations to the ground or to a leaf as part of their courtship."

Whether or not he is providing his own sonic accompaniment, he had better be good. "The courtship," adds Dr. Shear, "allows the female to be sure she is hooking up with a male of her own species. The ritual turns off the predatory instinct, so if the male does not do it exactly right, he gets treated like any other prey item."

This would take you out of the dating pool with, as they say, extreme prejudice. If the dance is accepted, the female wolf spider finds a safe place to spin a silk sheet on which she lays from fifty to two hundred eggs, something she may do two to four times in her two-year life span. She wraps them in a tough silk bundle she attaches to the rear of her abdomen, sometimes holding them aloft in the sun for warmth, perhaps to speed development.

She continues to hunt, carrying the eggs with her, becoming fiercer than ever, willing to defend them to the death. It's little wonder that one Spanish name for her is *buena madre,* or "good mother." In the spider world, she's as good as it gets. Hatching can take from two to eight weeks, with smaller species maturing more quickly. The mother tears the egg sac at its seams to release the hatchlings, which crawl onto her back and cling to knobs at the end of hairs until they mature, eating nothing and perhaps drinking dew.

For an attentive wildlife watcher, those egg sacs are a great way to know you're dealing with wolf spiders. Also known as ground or hunting spiders, they are common in the Southeast, and 50 or more of the world's 2,200 species live here. They vary from a half inch to four inches across, with stout bodies held close to the ground and long, hairy legs that are thicker and stronger than the spindly legs of many other spiders.

Up close, wolf spiders' eyes may be their most impressive features. They have relatively good vision, with four small eyes in a row on the bottom for close-ups and four larger eyes above—two for binocular vision and two farther back on the head for greater peripheral vision. The eyes reflect light like a cat's, and you can use a flashlight to find the creatures at night, when most are active.

Impressive, yes; attractive, no. Up close, a wolf spider looks like a bat with a ZZ Top beard and eyes like rows of hubcaps or headlights.

Their bodies are gray to brown, with patterns and color schemes that provide effective camouflage whatever their environment—grassy meadow, leaf litter on a forest floor, or the bank of a stream or pond. The camouflage, says Shear, "works best against birds, which are one of their main predators, but they are really at more risk from other spiders, which don't hunt by sight but by touch."

One of the most common, the Carolina wolf spider, *Hogna carolinensis*— the largest North American species—prefers wooded habitats and is, like most larger species, a burrowing spider, able to dig in almost any kind of soil and tending to stay with one burrow, enlarging it regularly.

Most wolf spiders, like about half of all spiders, don't build webs. Instead, they hunt insects like flies and crickets by stalking and pouncing—hence the group's name. They use their strong jaws to crush prey, then regurgitate softening enzymes and suck up the resultant soup.

"Most spiders are slow metabolizers that can go astonishingly long periods without feeding," says Shear. "Wolf spiders tend to be on the active side of that scale and will feed eagerly almost anytime. They will eat anything they can catch, including small frogs and lizards, insects, and spiders." They inject venom that can subdue relatively large prey, and their bites can be painful but aren't normally poisonous to humans—a good thing, since although they normally seek out crevices, leaf litter, or their burrows when it's cold or wet, they are found occasionally in human dwellings.

They are not a threat to us. Rather, as is usually the case, we are the threat to them, particularly where our farm and garden chemicals affect the prey they live on. This is a remarkable group of animals, and as wildlife watchers, we owe it to ourselves to appreciate a fascinating and often overlooked part of the world around us.

Wolf Spider

DESCRIPTION: From a half inch to 4 inches across; gray to brown; well camouflaged.

RANGE AND HABITAT: Fifty species in Southeast. It should be possible to find at least ten different species at any location in the Southeast, depending on habitat.

VIEWING TIPS: Hold a flashlight at eye level or use a headlamp, aiming the light about six to eight feet in front of you. The spider's eyes will appear like bright green sparks.

Black Rat Snake

In one corner of our yard, nestled amid coreopsis and calico asters that are breathtaking in the fall, sits a beat-up metal outbuilding designed to hold the lawn tractor, the garden tiller, and the yard tools. It's about the size of a low-slung one-car garage, so there has classically been room enough for occasional odds and ends we were going to deal with "any day now."

You might expect the odd hoses, wire, shingles, paint cans, empty feed bags, and cat carrier that clutter the walls and corners, and maybe even the smoker/grill and storm windows that have found their way inside. You might not expect the old kitchen sink in a big metal cabinet with six drawers and a lot of space underneath. It just sort of wound up there, and then lots of things, from tacks to gumboots, found their way into its roomy interior.

That old building has become one of the main hubs of activity in the yard. Mole passages crisscross its dirt floor. Skinks are common visitors.

Squirrels check for stored nuts, mice and birds build nests with some regularity, and I'll bet there's not an order of insect common to North America that hasn't had a representative crawl, hop, wriggle, or fly over, under, around, or through it.

The acknowledged royalty in this dilapidated domain generally enters silently and purposefully. It can glide easily to the most out-of-the-way nook from ground level to rooftop, and it won't hesitate to make a meal out of much of what's in there.

It is the black rat snake, a big, handsome reptile at the top of this particular shed's food chain. Sometimes our first sign of it in the spring is a papery skin lying behind the building—they shed from three to five times a year as they grow. More often, though, the birds will tell us when there's one about, fussing dramatically when one crosses the yard or climbs a tree looking for a nest, something that is doubly impressive at the upper range of its size, in the six- or seven-foot range.

"Rat snakes are the most common large snakes in suburban and other residential areas throughout their range in the southern states," says Whit Gibbons, professor emeritus of ecology at the University of Georgia. "As expert climbers, one is as likely to be found in a tree or shrub as on the ground. A snake in the attic or upper floors of a house is almost always a rat snake, and they will crawl under houses or outbuildings in search of rodents or as a refuge from hot or cold weather."

Their proximity means encounters with humans are not uncommon, and, unfortunately, rat snakes are mistaken all too often for rattlesnakes or copperheads by people unable or unwilling to know and appreciate the difference.

"Rat snakes make good neighbors," says Gibbons. "Nonvenomous and completely disinterested in making friends with humans, they rely on camouflage to go undetected and on a speedy retreat if discovered. All rat snakes prefer to spend their time resting out of sight or on a quest for a new meal."

Their prey includes rats and mice, voles, shrews, chipmunks, amphibians, and sometimes even squirrels and rabbits, as well as birds and their eggs.

"Rat snakes are superb hunters," says Gibbons, "whether searching high or low, night or day. Rats and mice are detected by scent, birds or their nests by sight. They are never in a hurry."

Sightings around chicken pens gave them the name "chicken snake," although they are generally after the rodents around a coop or, sometimes, eggs. They are not venomous but kill by constriction, biting to hold the animal, then wrapping around and suffocating it.

Breeding gets under way in April; then, in June or July, the female lays from five to thirty eggs in a rotten log or tree hole, in decaying leaf litter, or under a rock.

"The mother never looks back," says Gibbons. "Eggs and babies are on their own from the start." Those eggs, from one and a half to two inches long, "have an incubation time that averages around nine weeks but ranges from six to twelve. Nest site temperature affects the incubation period—the warmer the shorter." The hatchlings, from ten to thirteen inches long, begin appearing in late August or early September.

"In their first year after hatching," says Gibbons, "they nearly all look the same—a light gray body with darker gray blotches that will gradually fade. But among adults, the color pattern varies regionally. There are some that are solid black in the mountains and Piedmont regions, some with blotched patterns of black, gray, and brown in most areas, and olive-green or yellow with dark stripes in coastal areas of the Carolinas and most of Florida."

Active during the day in the spring and fall and at night during the summer, they go through a winter dormancy that is less extended in the Southeast than it can be farther north.

"Southern rat snakes do not undergo true hibernation," says Gibbons, "and can be active in southern areas during any season. A rat snake frequently will emerge from a refuge on warm winter days to bask in a sunny spot."

Though rat snakes are found quite often around people, like most other snakes they want to avoid us. If we do get near, they will often remain motionless, particularly as their color helps them remain invisible in a shadowed area. Approached too closely or handled, though, they will release a foul odor from scent glands, and if that isn't enough they'll bite, sometimes vigorously—a large one will inflict a painful bite that is likely to bleed profusely.

"A rat snake bite is an easy injury to avoid," says Gibbons. "Just don't pick it up!" While rat snakes are not venomous, it's worth updating a tetanus shot after a bite.

Like most other snakes, they will vibrate their tails when agitated, and if a snake this big does so in dry leaves or weeds, the similarity to the sound of a rattlesnake is enough to set a human nervous system on edge.

Young rat snakes are vulnerable to any number of predators, from hawks and owls to foxes, raccoons, opossums, and even neighborhood cats. Once they've reached adult size, few creatures will bother them. The exception, of course, is people, whose fear and ignorance often leave them unappreciative of and unconcerned about the fact that we're better off with them in places like our run-down old shed than we would be without them.

Black Rat Snake

DESCRIPTION: 7–8 feet maximum. Variety of color patterns, from solid black to olive-green or yellow with dark stripes.

RANGE AND HABITAT: Rat snakes are found throughout every southern state and have a broad geographic distribution that includes most of the eastern and midwestern states from New England through Florida west to Minnesota through Texas. Often around farms where rodents are abundant. Common in suburban areas in all southern states. Forest with nearby fields ideal.

VIEWING TIPS: Out at night in summer, during the day in the spring and fall.

Eastern Cottontail Rabbit

You've got to hand it to the rabbit. Few creatures have cut a wider swath through literature and culture than this meek, furry symbol of the reproductive arts. That connection has given us both the Easter bunny and the Playboy bunny, and the scope of the creature's wider influence can be seen in just a short list of its representatives in the culture—Thumper and Bugs, Br'er, Roger, and Peter Rabbit, *Alice in Wonderland*'s White Rabbit (and Jefferson

Airplane's psychedelic nod to it), the Velveteen Rabbit, Captain Kangaroo's Bunny Rabbit, and the hare (different genus, same family) who gets smoked by the tortoise.

What's not to love, right? Rabbits are docile, they're soft, and they have floppy ears and cottony tails. As an added bonus, they taste good.

Despite all that, rabbits have been known to stir negative emotions ranging from mild to homicidal. Ask any gardener. Better yet, ask the Aussies. Australia, whose evolutionary path branched off pretty early from the rest of the world's, has provided us with the quintessential be-careful what-you-let-loose story, and it involves the lowly rabbit.

In 1859, the year Charles Darwin published *On The Origin of Species,* an Australian farmer named Thomas Austin released twenty-four European rabbits on his property in southern Victoria as something to hunt. The rabbits reproduced like—well, like rabbits—and nothing had ever evolved on the continent to eat them, so there was no natural check on their population growth. Within ten years, hunters were taking two million rabbits a year without noticeably affecting their overall numbers. Meanwhile, the rabbits stripped vegetation to the extent that an undetermined number of plant species and some of the other mammals that fed on them went extinct.

Here in the Southeast, rabbits are not nearly as much of a problem, as they have quite a few natural predators—a long list that includes coyotes, bobcats, foxes, hawks, owls, large snakes, raccoons, crows, feral dogs and cats, and humans, as rabbits have long been one of the most abundantly taken small-game animals, and automobiles take quite a few as well. In fact, a rabbit's life expectancy isn't all that great here, with a year being about average, and much of that spent, as you might expect, in a wary mode.

Talk of population strength has to begin with habitat.

"The abundance of cottontails," says Rick Hamrick, wildlife biologist with the Mississippi Department of Wildlife, Fisheries, and Parks, "is largely a function of the amount of suitable cover and food in a given area. Given suitable habitat, they can quickly increase their numbers, even in the presence of a wide array of natural predators. Ideal rabbit habitat is characterized by a mixture of grassy cover and broadleaf herbs—some might say weeds or wildflowers, depending on your viewpoint—to feed, hide, and raise young, with patches of shrubby thickets for protective cover."

Rabbits were closely associated with the small farms once common throughout the South, but today's aggregated and intensive farming practices have often eliminated the field borders, dirty ditch banks, and hedgerows rabbits favor.

In uncultivated areas, says Hamrick, "Natural disturbances like fires, tornadoes, and floods are what naturally refresh and rejuvenate habitat for rabbits. In fact, activities like prescribed burning (closely supervised fires set intentionally under specific conditions) of grasslands and upland forests are an important management tool to enhance rabbit and other wildlife habitat."

Despite the challenges, the eastern cottontail rabbit remains widespread throughout much of the Southeast, occupying habitats ranging from old fields to woods and suburban areas. In portions of wetlands and bottomlands, it shares space with its relative the swamp rabbit, and the Appalachian cottontail and marsh rabbit are less-common relatives in parts of the Southeast.

The eastern cottontail can weigh from two to four pounds and is generally twelve to eighteen inches in length. It is grayish brown above, with grizzled black highlights and a whitish underside. The nape of the neck has a prominent reddish-brown patch, and there is sometimes a white blaze on the forehead. The rabbit molts twice a year and has a short summer coat and longer winter coat. Its rear feet are long and powerful, and its front feet act as shock absorbers.

Cottontails can be quite active at night, and at dawn and twilight. They nap or groom during the day, hiding in thickets or brush piles or under logs, although they often emerge on overcast days.

A rabbit's defensive strategies, important given all those predators, are paradoxical. On one hand, there is that storied speed. A rabbit can leap fifteen feet at a clip and can hit eighteen miles per hour, zigzagging as it dashes for cover. On the other end of the spectrum, there's motionlessness. A rabbit can remain still for fifteen minutes, becoming all but invisible in tall grass. It can also slink away, staying low and keeping its ears laid back to avoid detection. Rabbits will rise on their hind feet to search for danger and thump their feet to indicate its arrival. They can also produce a loud, shrill scream.

"Rabbits have keen vision, hearing, and sense of smell," says Hamrick. "Like many prey animals, their eyes are positioned such that they have a wide field of vision—they can see in nearly all directions—and they will use all of these senses to size up impending danger."

They themselves, of course, are a threat only to vegetation. They are particularly fond of clover, the leaves and seeds of small grains such as wheat and oats, as well as bluegrass, dandelions, plantain, lamb's quarter, lespedeza, crabgrass, and ragweed. When it comes to gardens, they will eat peas, beans, lettuce, and carrots, among others. In the winter, they will turn to hay, as well as bark, twigs, seeds, and roots, and so are of as much concern to foresters and orchard growers as they are to summer gardeners.

It's obvious their diet can provide plenty of nutrients, and rabbits have a way to maximize what they take in.

"The technical term," says Hamrick, "is *coprophagia*—the consumption of feces. Rabbits produce hard and soft fecal pellets [the soft ones are greener and less thoroughly digested], and they can consume the soft pellets to extract nutrients not absorbed the first time through."

Their storied mating prowess shows another side of them. For all their seeming calm and timidity, according to Hamrick, "Breeding brings out the aggressiveness in males, which will fight each other, with the dominant buck driving off the others. The male will then display for females, which are terri torial during breeding season; males are not. The male will chase the female, then she will stop and face him and box at him with her front paws. Either or both may leap into the air in a dance that leads to copulation."

Late in her twenty-eight-day gestation, the female begins clearing a nest in a hollow in tall grass or under a shrub or log, lining it with grass and fur from her breast and belly. The young (generally four or five, although anywhere from one to nine are possible) are born blind, naked, and helpless.

They feed from four pairs of mammaries, and in a week they have fur and can see. They are weaned between sixteen and twenty-two days. At seven weeks they disperse, and the female is often about to give birth again as the current litter leaves the nest. They mature at four months or so and may breed before their first winter, although most breed the following spring. In the southernmost parts of the Southeast, they can breed year-round, with their populations cycling in response to weather, predator abundance, and changes in habitat conditions.

Rabbits do carry diseases, most of which are not human health concerns. One, though, tularemia, a bacterial disease, can be life threatening to humans, although transmission from rabbit to human is rare and the disease is treatable with antibiotics when diagnosed early.

For the average wildlife watcher, though, rabbits are benign creatures whose positives, culturally, aesthetically, and culinarily, far outweigh their bad points. Unless, perhaps, you're a gardener or an Aussie.

Eastern Cottontail Rabbit

DESCRIPTION: 15–18 inches in length; 3 pounds; gray-brown, long ears, large hind feet, cottony tail.

RANGE AND HABITAT: Grass, fields, clearings, prairies, and open woodlands with shrubs for cover.

VIEWING TIPS: Keep watch in grassy areas, especially mornings and evenings.

Groundhog

We've got a yard you might call rough around the edges. The woods threaten constantly to encroach another foot or so toward the house. The weeds always seem to be getting just a little higher around the gardens. Brush piles dot the perimeters like turrets on a castle wall, and the circles of uncut grass around some of the trees widen a tad each year.

We wouldn't trade it. There's no telling how many hours of toil we've been spared over the years by letting just one additional swipe of green escape the lawn tractor. More important, there have been rewards everywhere— dove and quail nests, fox and rabbit sightings, skunks, raccoons, owls, black rat snakes, and much, much more—not to mention the wildflowers nestled in among all those gangly stalks.

Some of my favorite yard-edge denizens are the groundhogs. We'll spot them at the edge of the grass in the evening now and then, earnest and lumpy in the still air, ambling gracelessly toward hidden dens. Sometimes they'll squat amid the weeds, munching clover or plantain or some other favorite, a wary eye cast about for potential trouble. And then there are the unexpected treats such as the times we spot breath clouds rising from den holes after sudden cold snaps.

The groundhog, which is what most people call them, or woodchuck, an alteration of their Algonquin name that is used in most of the scientific literature, looks on the surface to be sweet and cuddly, a big, padded, bushy-tailed cousin to its relatives in the family Sciuirdae, which include ground and tree squirrels, chipmunks, and marmots. But, while it might seem to be our answer to the panda or koala bear, like them, it is not all sweetness and light.

"Their looks can be deceiving," says Dr. Chris Maher, professor of biology at the University of Southern Maine. "Despite their excellent ability to habituate to humans and tolerate urban or suburban settings, they are still wild animals."

Her years of experience live-trapping them for study have given her the kind of hands-on experience few of us will ever have—and knowledge that these loose-skinned rodents come in a variety of personality types.

"When I handle them," she says, "always using a cone-shaped cloth handling bag to protect the woodchuck as well as myself and my students, they may stay perfectly still as I weigh them, mark them on the back and rump with nontoxic hair dye, and place numbered tags in their ears so I can recognize them again. Or they may fight me every step of the way, squirming inside the bag or turning around continuously, which just prolongs the process. We make sure to keep our fingers away from their heads, because not only are their teeth sharp and jaws strong but they can be quick! I've been nipped through a Kevlar-lined handling glove, and I still feel a painful pinch."

Predators (and other groundhogs) know to be wary as well.

"I once watched a juvenile woodchuck fend off an immature red-tailed hawk," says Maher. "Neither one seemed too sure of its role in the relationship. When the hawk swooped down toward the woodchuck pup, it flipped onto its back and brandished its claws at the hawk, which landed on the ground nearby. As the hawk hopped toward the woodchuck, the pup went on the offensive, growling and lunging at the hawk. It seemed to be a draw, and we'll never know who would have won because the staff naturalist at the time stepped in to break up the standoff."

Groundhogs' jaws and incisors, like those of other rodents, are extremely powerful, designed as they are for cutting, tearing, and chewing vegetation, and they can be turned quite effectively on a predator. Their front feet, which are powerful digging tools, can also inflict damage. Coyotes, foxes, bobcats, and roaming dogs learn to avoid the business end of a groundhog, which can inflict nasty bites, and they know especially not to corner it. The most effective predation technique is to use stealth to catch the groundhog unawares.

Most often, a groundhog will zip toward its burrow, throwing itself down an inconspicuous drop hole that may be two feet deep, then crawling into a maze of tunnels that may run forty feet in length and get to be eight or ten feet deep. Those dens usually have several entrances. The primary one, which Maher calls "the porch," is surrounded by a mound of dirt and is used as a lookout, or, as Maher says, "to bask or doze in the sun or shade, depending on time of day and location."

"Woodchucks can bring up an impressive amount of soil [as much as hundreds of pounds] in a short period of time, using their heads as shovels to push the soil away from the entrance," she says. "As they disappear back underground to continue digging, I've seen the dirt flying out of the opening as they kick it back, until they're too deep for the dirt to clear the surface. It's amusing to watch."

A single woodchuck may have four or five dens in its territory. Summer dens may be shallow and situated near thick vegetation suitable for foraging, and winter dens may be deeper and protected, perhaps by woods or brush piles. They are particularly fond of patches of kudzu, since they'll eat it and it provides great cover.

Woodchucks fertilize and aerate the soil. Their burrows also serve as refuge for rabbits, raccoons, foxes, snakes, opossums, chipmunks, mice, and many others. They can, of course, be pests to farmers and gardeners, feeding on tomatoes, lettuce, and other plants.

Groundhogs are true hibernators, a fact that has helped give rise to the tale of Groundhog Day, personified these days by Pennsylvania's Punxsutawney Phil, who emerges every year on February 2 to make a weather prediction. If he sees his shadow, there will be six more weeks of winter. The legend has its origins in Europe, where badgers were the prognosticators of choice at the halfway point between the winter solstice and the spring equinox.

"When settlers came to the eastern part of North America," says Maher, "they substituted woodchucks." In the Southeast, the cold generally isn't deep enough or long-lasting enough to necessitate long-term hibernation, and they'll emerge when there's warmth and available food.

A 2009 study led by Stam Zervanos of Penn State, looking at three years' data, showed that woodchucks in South Carolina on average hibernated from December 12 until February 26, going into torpor, a usually brief and involuntary period of slowed metabolism, an average of eleven times. In Pennsylvania the dates were November 14 through March 1, with fifteen instances of torpor, and in southern Maine from October 18 through April 3, with twenty bouts of torpor. Individuals in all three populations lost an average of a third of their body weight during that overall period of hibernation.

Mating begins in earnest in March or so with the return of warmer weather. Competing males will square off, hissing, growling, and chattering, and their fights will sometimes leave serious scars. Males will then search for and enter the nest of a female.

"Courtship," says Maher, "includes vocalizations by the male—soft cooing or churring noises. Usually, you have to be very close to hear them, as when you walk up to a burrow and a male and female are inside. A male will raise his tail vertically and move it back and forth slowly [it's called tail flagging] and sniff around her rump. She usually ignores him, chases him, snaps at him, or avoids him by disappearing into the burrow." Copulation may occur above or below ground, and the female will mate with more than one male.

"Different males sire offspring within the same litter," says Maher. "Juveniles that are littermates can be full siblings or half siblings."

The groundhog's gestation period is about thirty-one days, with first-time mothers typically giving birth to two or three naked, blind, and helpless pups under four inches in length, a number that rises to four or five per litter thereafter. Pups can walk at a little more than three weeks of age, with weaning and their first tentative journeys from the nest at about four weeks. "The young weigh about one pound when they first emerge above ground," says Maher, "and they are really clueless. They don't stray too far from the burrow at first but gradually venture farther away. If they are threatened and far enough from a burrow, they freeze, which could work well as a defensive move in tall grass where a predator might not see them."

Besides four-legged predators, they are susceptible to hunting and run-ins with autos, and severe winters or flooded burrows can take their toll as well. The young are often taken by snakes and hawks.

Those that make it, says Maher, "don't always leave home in their first year. Some of them stick around, and their mothers tolerate their presence. Mom may chase them around, but some manage to resist her efforts and stay put. In some cases, they can remain in their natal territory for life—like a forty-year-old living in his parents' basement!"

Those that do venture away from home can have a rough time of it, as they will be driven away from other groundhogs' territories and their movement can make them more susceptible to highway encounters. It's the same when it comes to relocation by humans.

"I try to discourage people from trapping and moving woodchucks elsewhere," says Maher. "People think they're being humane; however, they don't stop to consider that they've just deposited the woodchuck in a completely foreign land where it doesn't know where burrows are located. It may encounter other woodchucks that chase the intruder out of the territory, and as it moves, it could encounter predators, with no place to escape, or cars as it tries to cross roads in an effort to find a place to live or get away from territory owners."

Still, this is one of the few species that has flourished because of humans. The clearing of the eastern forests made for a lot more of the meadows and forest edges they prefer. Now, though, we are removing habitat as we pave over meadows for housing subdivisions and strip malls.

In those places where groundhogs are found, primarily in the northern half of the Southeast, people are of two minds about them.

"Theirs is an uneasy relationship with humans," says Maher. "Some people love having them in the yard, and others (for example, many gardeners) despise them. And it's hard to make woodchucks understand that the smorgasbord of vegetables laid out before them is not meant for them to eat!"

Debby and I are gardeners. We are also lovers of the groundhog. We believe in a rough-around-the-edges lawn, and we believe good garden fences make good neighbors. There is something about watching a groundhog placidly munching plantain on a summer evening that contributes greatly to the bucolic setting we call home. We heed the advice we would give anyone in the country—keep them out of the bean patch and welcome these charming, burrowing denizens of the forest edge.

Groundhog

DESCRIPTION: Up to 2 feet long, 6-inch tail; about 10 pounds in the fall, half that in the spring, after hibernation. Brown, furry, short, round ears, sharp teeth, digging claws.

RANGE AND HABITAT: Forest edges, farms, and pastures. Much of eastern North America and Midwest, across Canada to Alaska. Mostly northern half of Southeast.

VIEWING TIPS: Evenings are a great time to look for groundhogs at yard edges.

Red Fox

When we moved to our little white house in the country, fields and woods teeming with wildlife sprawled in every direction. We heard whippoorwills and watched quail scurry across the back yard. There were deer and turkeys and four kinds of owls.

Then, slowly, inexorably, the city crept toward us. A convenience market here, a subdivision there, and then a Walmart. Finally, hundreds of acres of great birding four miles away gave way to a huge commercial and residential development, and we knew the countryside had been changed forever.

One overcast autumn evening as I stood in the yard, a red fox trotted across a field behind the house. It stopped not twenty yards away, ears cocked, and we stared at each other.

This was a striking creature, amber eyes set amid orange-red fur that gave way to white on the chin and chest above dark stockings on long forelegs. I hoped I was not looking at the last fox I would see this close to the house, but I knew with every fiber of my being to treasure the moment. Finally, he relaxed and trotted off, but to this day that fox remains a vivid symbol of that mysterious bond we share with the wild creatures around us and of the awful chasm between us. We are kindred and we are other.

Given the effect that fox had on me, I never wonder about the hold they have on the human imagination. Foxes can be found from Aesop to Grimm, in the Old and New Testaments, and in myth and folklore around the world. They are portrayed as cunning and deceitful, wise and treacherous, attributes reflecting our respect for their intelligence and adaptability.

We have hunted them for millennia, in part because of that respect, as they present a real challenge to sport hunters. Much of the reason, though, lies in their taste for game we crave and in our desire for their fur.

Real opportunists, red foxes will eat anything from insects to carrion, and while the bulk of their diet consists of mice and voles, they eat enough game birds, squirrels, and rabbits to earn the enmity of many hunters. Then there is their affinity for chickens and turkeys—they will kill more than they consume, so they might well lay waste to a henhouse—and the fact that they sometimes kill calves, lambs, and piglets. Long considered nuisance animals, they have had bounties on their heads in many states.

We took them too because we found them attractive. Their fur, thick, long, silky, has long been sought for warmth and fashion, and there remains an active market for trappers and ranchers worldwide.

"Red fox fur, including the northern color variations of silver, black, and cross fox, has always been a top fashion item in the fur trade," says Jim Spencer, an outdoor author, editor, hunter, and trapper from Arkansas. "The wild fur market has been in a slump since 2014, but prime, quality red fox fur is still in demand. Buyers in China and Russia drive most of the wild fur market, and when the economies of these countries improve, so will the demand for red fox and other wild furs."

Small and slender, though still the largest of the foxes, the red fox stands fourteen to eighteen inches at the shoulder and weighs from eight to fourteen pounds. From twenty to twenty-six inches long, it has a bushy, ten- to fifteen-inch tail used for balance, for warmth in winter, and for signaling everything from aggression to danger, something it also does with a variety of barks, howls, yips, and growls, along with facial and posture cues. Barks and screams, thought to announce territory and communicate with partners, have been described as "disturbingly human."

That red fur is just the most common color phase for the species, but all the phases have white-tipped tails that help distinguish them from the slightly smaller gray fox and from larger coyotes and wolves.

Red foxes, native to much of Europe and Asia, moved to North America across the Bering land bridge between 130,000 and 300,000 years ago, then expanded their range across the continent between 130,000 and 100,000 years ago.

"They were likely limited," says Bryant White, Furbearer Research Program Manager with the Association of Fish and Wildlife Agencies, "to a range of boreal and mixed hardwood forest habitats north of 40 to 45 degrees, based on archaeological evidence." They moved in the twentieth century from Canada into the central and eastern states, while nonnative red foxes were being introduced from Europe for hunting, expanding their range dramatically. They are present now throughout almost all of the southern states with the exception of southern Florida, with their preferred habitat being agricultural areas interspersed with wooded tracts. They are increasingly drawn to suburban areas where there is a diversity of woodlots and open space.

"In the past couple of decades," says Spencer, "the eastern encroachment of coyotes has impacted red fox populations. Not only do coyotes compete directly with red foxes for available food, they actively prey on foxes. This has caused reds to become even more a species of the suburbs; they use humans as protection from coyotes." While numbers are hard to come by, monitoring through fur harvest records and scent station data indicates a decline in red fox populations more or less nationwide, although, White adds, "The harvest fluctuates with market demand, and the market is pretty low right now, so harvests would be lower."

The mating process brings these normally solitary creature together, and they often form lasting pair bonds. They begin courtship in late fall or early winter, traveling and hunting together for three weeks or so.

They excavate or expand on natal dens, including those of groundhogs and skunks, which can be fifteen to twenty feet in length, with a side passage or two. Gestation takes from fifty-one to fifty-three days, and a vixen will give birth to four to eight kits in March or April. The young are born blind and deaf, weighing just two to three ounces, and though they have fur, they must rely on their mother, who rarely leaves the den for weeks after giving birth, for warmth. The kits' eyes open at ten days or so and they begin spending time outside the den at about a month. They nurse for another two or three weeks, until the parents begin regurgitating solid food for them, eventually bringing live mice and moles so they can practice their hunting skills—stalking, pouncing, and killing.

They travel in family groups through the summer, supplementing their diets with fruit and berries, and the young grow to adult size by the fall, with both sexes reaching sexual maturity by about ten months. Sometimes one or more of the young will remain with the female into the next year, assisting the male in providing for the female while she is in the den nursing.

Kits are taken by hawks and owls as well as coyotes, and both adults and young are killed by automobiles. Foxes are susceptible to mange and rabies as well; in fact, statistics indicate that red foxes are one of the animals most likely to be the source of an attack by a rabid wild animal.

The red fox's continued journey from rural to suburban and urban centers means our exposure to them may well increase. It took years, but I've seen foxes again, and trail cameras offer regular and heartening confirmation that they're still around, or perhaps that they've reversed their retreat. Still, I never take for granted that they'll be here next week or next year. Amid the deer and raccoons, the turkeys and owls, the red fox is something special, especially since the quail and whippoorwills have gone. I'll continue to treasure it.

Red Fox

DESCRIPTION: 7–14 pounds, 3–4 feet in length including long white-tipped tail. Striking red color, although there are silver, black and "cross" phases.
RANGE AND HABITAT: Adaptable, but prefers open space with cover, mixed open/wooded terrain. Found through much of North America and most of the Southeast, particularly in agricultural areas, except in southern Florida. Increasing presence in suburbs and even urban areas.
VIEWING TIPS: Early mornings and late evenings best. Some daylight presence, especially when kits are young.

Eastern Mole

Let's call him Ed. He was our neighbor in the '90s, and he was, to be sure, not a wildlife watcher. In his worldview, everything was out to raid his garden, ruin his lawn, or kill him. Weeds were to be eradicated, and if what he used ran off and fouled waterways, well, that was the way it was. Every snake was a copperhead, deserving of death. This was a man with free time, set ways, and plenty of patience, and all of that came together quite dramatically in the case of moles. Dissatisfied with the traps proffered by Tractor Supply and home remedies like cayenne pepper and mothballs, he would tamp down the freshest tunnel in his yard, pull up a lawn chair and a .45, and wait silently. A window-rattling "blam!" let us know when one more mole had been reduced to airborne components.

We, on the other hand, have never minded them. They may be the bane of those who like picture-perfect lawns and golf courses, but it would be difficult to overstate their importance to the soil, and, at least out in the country, picture-perfect is overrated.

"Moles," says Dr. Gregory Hartman, professor of biology at Georgia's Gordon State College, "provide soils and soil ecosystems with aeration, physical turnover, the movement and cycling of nutrients, and the dispersal of mycorrhizal fungi." The latter, in symbiotic relationship with plants, allow for increased absorption of water and nutrients.

Far more than soil benefits from the churning and tunneling. "Mole tunnel systems," adds Hartman, "are used as travel corridors and/or places of refuge by a variety of invertebrate animals and vertebrates including shrews, voles, snakes, lizards, salamanders, frogs, and toads." That's a lot of benefit from an animal that, in the case of the eastern mole, is six inches long and weighs just three ounces.

The mole is a digging machine, perfectly suited to underground travel. It uses a swimming motion, its big, pink, outward-facing front feet, with toes tipped in sturdy claws, churning through dirt like mechanized coal-diggers, pushing soil up and to the sides when making surface tunnels and under and behind itself as it creates and travels through deeper tunnels. Its robust foreleg, shoulder, and breast bones anchor powerful muscles that drive those feet, enabling it to dig at four and a half meters an hour, or an inch every fifteen seconds. It's got a sensitive and relatively naked tail to help guide it in backing up and velvety fur that can lie flat in either direction so as not to impede motion.

You'd be hard-pressed to detect sense organs. The eyelids are fused over the tiny eyes, which are just sensitive enough to tell light from dark. Although moles have good hearing, their ears are hidden under their fur. The snout, long, relatively naked and pink, has sensory whiskers and nostrils that open upward.

Overall, moles look for the same things we do in soil. "Eastern moles," says Hartman, "seem to prefer sandy and loamy soils, and to avoid heavy clay soils." They're looking for abundant food, as constant digging is a high-energy operation. A mole will consume about half its weight per day, feeding on earthworms, slugs, snails, centipedes, cutworms, insects and their larvae (including undesirables like Japanese beetles), and occasionally some seeds. The surface tunnels we see are essentially dining runs, and they are just the upper chambers of an elaborate subway system. They are connected to a permanent set of passageways a foot or so underground providing habitation, relief from heat or cold (moles do not hibernate), and, in the spring, a nest/nursery. Sometimes the central den will be under a tree, shrub, stump, or rock—or, for that matter, a sidewalk or patio. In excavating those tunnels, the mole will pile dirt at above-ground locations above vertical shafts—your basic molehill.

"The dynamics of tunnel usage (surface or deep) really have not been studied very much," says Hartman. "We do know that one mole will use the abandoned tunnels of another; this makes some sense when you consider the expenditure of energy required to construct a tunnel. One particular tunnel in South Carolina that I kept track of still was in use after ten years."

As moles dig, they secrete from oil glands a musky substance thought to discourage predators, mark territory, and serve as a sexual signal. It also stains their fur, leaving brownish yellow patches.

The Eastern mole's Linnaean name is worth notice here. *Scalopus* means "digging foot," and it's perfectly in order. *Aquaticus* means "found in water," and it shows Linnaeus didn't always hit it on the head. He found one dead in the water, took note of the webbed feet, and erroneously assumed a connection.

Being underground is an excellent defense mechanism, although moles are above ground some of the time and some creatures will take the time to dig them up. They fall prey to owls and hawks, foxes and coyotes, cats and dogs, and, as someone who has raised chickens, I can tell you now and then a chicken will dig one up and kill it. Then, of course, there are snakes, which can follow them into their burrows. And they are parasite magnets, with fleas, lice, and mites all dogging them.

Moles have home ranges, averaging about two and a half acres for males and three-quarters of an acre for females, with wide variation depending the quality of soil—in great soil you can find several per acre.

The mating process gets under way in spring, when, says Hartman, "males enlarge their home ranges. Sometimes this involves extending tunnel systems, traveling aboveground, or both." Once he finds a female and mates, he moves on to find another. The female builds a spherical nest chamber lined with dry plant material. After a gestation of about forty-five days, she gives birth to three or four young, as early as March in warm climates and as late as June farther north.

The young are naked and blind, developing at ten days a fine velvety fur that lasts for several weeks until their regular fur grows in. The female, who has six teats, nurses them, and they are weaned and can leave the nest at about a month and can fend for themselves in another week or two—in fact, the mother may forcibly disperse them. The young establish their own home ranges and tunnel systems, usually not far from maternal burrows, and reach sexual maturity the following spring.

Those new tunnel systems may well appear where you are. Our former neighbor notwithstanding, we'd do well to appreciate them and cut them some slack. A great lawn looks as good to a mole as it does to you, and if you've got moles, it simply means you're doing good work.

Eastern Mole

DESCRIPTION: Large claws; silver-brown fur above, paler underneath. Length 6 inches, weight 3 ounces; male slightly larger than female.
RANGE AND HABITAT: Native to eastern U.S. In good soil throughout the Southeast, except southern Florida.
VIEWING TIPS: Look for telltale surface tunnel ridges and/or mounds.

Copperhead

After eons of brain development, you'd think that as a species we would be a little brighter. But just when I begin to hope we've turned a corner, I have only to read the paper or watch the news to be brought back to reality. Let's just say it's apparent we don't always have our thinking caps on.

Given what we know about venomous snakes, for instance, shouldn't people be aware that the best strategy is simply to give them a wide berth?

That, unfortunately, is not always the case, particularly for those of us equipped with Y-chromosomes.

The figures are sketchy, but it's apparent that a goodly number of snake-bites are due to—well, let's call it a regrettable lack of perspicacity. As a case in point, consider a friend of mine. He was at a backyard family cookout, serenely fulfilling his role as designated drinker. Toward evening, his young son saw a snake at the edge of the yard. Viewing this as the perfect educational opportunity, my friend proceeded to talk to his boy about the differences between venomous and nonvenomous snakes.

"Son," he said, "this is obviously not a venomous snake." He set his beer down, grabbed a long stick from the edge of the woods, and managed to pin the snake against the grass. Then he picked it up. The snake, acting as I would have, bit him on the forearm. Meanwhile, friends and relatives had by then spotted a prominent field mark—the snake's copper-colored head.

We will get to the science in a moment, but I can tell you from the layman's point of view what happened to my friend's arm over the next several days. Basically, it turned dark and swelled until it was thicker than his leg, and then the skin split like that of an overripe tomato. My friend reported that the pain and throbbing were beyond belief. He threw up a lot, and his blood pressure dropped to the point that he was hospitalized. He has since been a lot more circumspect around all manner of reptiles. The scar is still impressive.

There are several lessons here, although I don't feel the need to spell them out. I will say, however, that if you're going to get bitten by a venomous snake, you could do worse than the copperhead.

"One reason for favorable odds if you're bitten by a southern copperhead rather than a cottonmouth or rattlesnake," says Whit Gibbons, professor emeritus of ecology at the University of Georgia and author of *Snakes of the Southeast*, "is their comparatively low venom potency drop for drop. A bite from an adult timber or diamondback rattler is likely to be ten times or more as dangerous as an average copperhead bite."

The lower toxicity of copperhead venom is a good thing, as this is a very common snake throughout much of the eastern United States, even though most of us remain blissfully unaware of them.

"Within their geographic range," says Gibbons, "copperheads generally avoid aquatic habitats but could be almost anywhere else and go unseen. Their leaflike patterns of brown and tan make them virtually invisible to a person walking in a forest. Without question, copperheads see far more hikers and hunters each year than either see copperheads. The same is often true in suburban areas, where copperheads may be more common than the human inhabitants. They hide in plain sight not only from the few enemies, including people, that might attack them, but are also concealing themselves from the potential meals of mice, lizards, or frogs that might happen by." They've been known, interestingly enough, to eat cicadas when they emerge in the summer.

The fact that we don't often spot them is in great part due to their fervent desire to avoid us.

"Venom is a precious meal ticket for a copperhead," says Gibbons, "and only to be wasted biting a person as a last resort. In fact, most bites by copperheads are warning shots and inject little or no venom, another reason for the low incidence of serious bites to people."

Copperheads are not among our larger venomous snakes, with a four-foot specimen being in the upper range. They have triangular heads, elliptical eyes, and heat-sensitive pits between their eyes and nostrils to detect objects warmer than their surroundings—like prey. They are tan to pinkish red, with chestnut-colored, hourglass-shaped bands across the back and sides and a lighter belly.

They are generally ambush predators, lying in wait for prey. They will eat rodents, birds, frogs, and other snakes, although up to 90 percent of their diet consists of mice and voles. Their venom contains cytotoxins and hemotoxins, which cause tissue damage and hemorrhaging, as well as the swelling and pain that made my friend's life so miserable. They will bite and hold smaller prey and bite and release larger animals, tracking them until the poison slows and kills them. The lower jawbone is really two bones attached by tendons, giving copperheads the ability to stretch their throats wide enough to swallow prey up to twice their own diameter.

Females give birth in the fall, but copperheads may mate in either the spring or fall, with the female able to store sperm until the following spring, at which time maturing eggs are fertilized. They are ovoviviparous, an intermediate form between viviparous (live-bearing) and oviparous (egg-laying), with a female giving birth to four to seven live young that hatched from eggs while still in her body. The young look a great deal like adults except that their tails are bright yellow, and immature copperheads use those tails as lures to attract prey. As each grows, it sheds its skin from one to three times a year, more often while young and growing rapidly. Both sexes reach sexual maturity at about four years of age, when they are about two feet long, and they can live up to twenty years.

Copperheads are active during the day except in the hottest parts of the summer, when they become primarily nocturnal. While many snakes in northern climates seek communal dens in cold winter weather, much of the South's climate is mild enough that copperheads will generally ride out cold weather in stump holes and burrows. A rocky outcropping on a cool day isn't a bad place to look for them, since copperheads will sun themselves when the opportunity arises.

But keep your distance. More people in the United States are bitten by copperheads than by any other venomous snake, and a little common sense would help reduce the number of such incidents. Copperheads give off warnings when threatened, including a distinctive musk that smells like cucumber. Keeping encounters from getting to that point is not that complicated.

"As with all venomous snakes," says Gibbons, "the best course of action upon encountering one is to calmly move out of striking range and mind your own business. Take a photograph. Enjoy the show. A copperhead wants nothing to do with us, but, if cornered or pestered, it will defend itself. Don't offer yourself as a target by getting too close and certainly not by picking one up."

That, of course, is a lesson my friend the designated drinker no doubt wishes he had learned by means other than personal experience. I, for one, am glad I was able to learn by observation.

Copperhead

DESCRIPTION: Up to 4 feet long; copper-colored head; striped hour-glass markings.

RANGE AND HABITAT: Generalist. Can be found from sandhills to swamp edges, from deep woods to suburban areas. Most of the Southeast except the Florida peninsula.

VIEWING TIPS: Rocky outcrops are particularly favorable.

Bobcat

We need look no further than fairy tales to grasp the enmity Europeans had for predators. Wolves took the brunt of it, since lions, which once roamed widely across southern Europe, had for the most part disappeared by the first century AD. (Bears were extinct in England and in retreat elsewhere in Europe by the same time.) Classic fairy tales, such as *The Three Little Pigs* and *Little Red Riding Hood,* with their roots in the oral traditions of early European societies, and the Greek fable *The Little Boy Who Cried Wolf* all attest to the wolf's sway on the early human imagination.

When European settlers arrived in the New World, the vast North American continent was as rich with predators as it was with other flora and fauna. The larger ones often took livestock, and settlers began hunting, trapping, poisoning, and otherwise working to eradicate them. It took centuries, but the eastern mountain lion was declared extinct in the wild in 2013. A subspecies, the Florida panther, which once roamed from Arkansas to the Carolinas, is represented by perhaps two hundred individuals in southern Florida. The red wolf was declared extinct in the wild in 1980 (a nonessential experimental population of a few dozen roams a small portion of eastern North Carolina now).

But one of the smaller predators native to the Southeast, the bobcat, has used its inborn stealth and wariness to survive into the twenty-first century, though it has not been easy.

"Like most predators that competed with man for food, bobcats were killed with near impunity due to their potential as predators of game and livestock," says Jay Butfiloski, supervisor for the South Carolina Department of Natural Resources' Furbearer Project, "probably up through the time that the region really began to transition away from being primarily an agrarian society."

It is estimated, though, that there are now between 2.3 and 3.6 million bobcats throughout its range. A decline in the popularity of hunting bobcats is no doubt one factor. Regulated hunting is thought to account for about half of bobcat deaths annually, with automobiles contributing as well. There is a legal trade in bobcat skins, and in 2015 more than sixty-five thousand were exported. Bobcats are also susceptible to diseases, including scabies, and to poisoning by way of eating poisoned rats or mice. As with many creatures, habitat loss and fragmentation are major concerns.

Bobcats are supremely adaptable, with twelve subspecies living everywhere from Florida swamps to southwestern deserts and from southern Canada to northern Mexico. They can be found in the most remote wilderness and in our suburbs and even cityscapes. They are found in forty-seven of the contiguous states, excluding only Delaware. A 2011 analysis in the *Journal of Fish and Wildlife Management* confirmed that the species' population had increased since the 1990s, and, according to the International Society for Endangered Cats Canada, population density in the Southeast for the bobcat ranges from eleven per one hundred square kilometers in Virginia to forty-eight in Texas.

"In some midwestern states," says Bryant White, Furbearer Research Program Manager with the Association of Fish and Wildlife Agencies, "their populations have increased as much as 300 percent since the 1990s. In fact, several states in the Midwest are now allowing hunting/trapping seasons that had not previously had them, and other states have liberalized harvest. While there are no solid answers as to why the population has so dramatically increased, I think everyone is glad to see it because they are beautiful and amazing animals."

The bobcat is indeed a marvelous predator, combining stealth with power and quick acceleration. Bobcats prefer rabbits and other small mammals, but they can and will eat anything from insects to deer. They are a significant predator of fawns, stalking from cover or lying in wait to pounce. A bobcat can kill prey ten times its size, and it will cover what it can't eat with leaves. It is also legendarily elusive. Even now, with its population "quite secure," according to Butfiloski, sighting one is an extraordinarily rare occurrence.

One of four lynx species (the Canada, Eurasian, and Iberian lynx are the others), the bobcat is about twice the size of an average domestic cat, from thirty to forty inches in length, with a bobbed, black-tipped tail that gives it its common name. It stands, on average, between sixteen and twenty-two inches at the shoulder, with males weighing eighteen to thirty pounds and females fourteen to twenty-two. Bobcats have gray to brown coats (reddish in summer), with lighter underbellies. Black spots, with dark bars on the forelegs, are typical. Bobcats also have yellow eyes and black-tufted ears ("The tufts are a key indicator that what you are looking at is actually a bobcat and not a large feral house cat," says Butfiloski), sensitive whiskers, and fur "ruffs" under their ears, along their cheeks, that make their faces look wider.

Bobcats are active mostly at dusk and dawn, patrolling a territory that can vary widely in size depending on their sex (males and females may share overlapping territories), the terrain, and food availability, with scrapings and scent markings defining its boundaries. Each bobcat will have a main den and several secondary shelters in thickets, brush piles, or hollow logs. During fall and winter, they, like their prey, become more active during the day. They have voracious appetites, a good sense of smell, and great hearing and vision; the number of rats, mice, and rabbits eaten by a single female bobcat and three kittens per year can number in the thousands.

Peak breeding season for bobcats is February and March. A male and female will travel and hunt together for a few days, engaging in chasing and bumping behavior sometimes accompanied by great throaty growls—the bobcat's vocalizations can have an other-worldly tenor. Both males and females may mate several times with different partners.

After two months of gestation, the female will select a secluded spot and give birth to two to four young weighing around three-quarters of a pound each. Their eyes open by day ten; they begin exploring at a month and are weaned at two months. Their mother will bring them birds and small mammals and begin teaching them to kill. They start traveling at three to five months and will be hunting on their own by the fall. By the time the female mates again the following winter, the previous year's young will be on their own.

The young bobcats are vulnerable to virtually any carnivore, including birds of prey and even adult male bobcats. The process of going out on their own, perfecting hunting techniques, and establishing individual territories is fraught with peril, and juveniles have high mortality rates. They are susceptible to ticks and fleas, as well as internal parasites, some of which they pick up from rabbits and squirrels.

In truth, humans don't have much at all to fear from bobcats. Irrational fear has doomed some other predators, but the bobcat's wariness of humans has worked to its advantage. Their ghostly presence throughout the Southeast may go unnoticed by most of us, but the bobcat remains one of our most precious wildlife treasures.

Bobcat

DESCRIPTION: Gray to brown, with facial and ear tufts, bars on the forelegs and spots otherwise. Length is 30–40 inches; stands 16–22 inches at shoulder; weighs 14–30 pounds.
RANGE AND HABITAT: Adaptable. Primarily deciduous or coniferous woods but can be found from swamps to scrubland and in suburban areas. Southern Canada to northern Mexico. Throughout the Southeast.
VIEWING TIPS: Secluded wooded areas at dusk or daylight. Bobcats are more active in the daytime in winter. This is a highly elusive creature. For those who wish to spot them, learning to look for tracks, scat, or markings is helpful.

Earthworm

Many plants and animals we take for granted weren't part of the landscape that greeted the first Europeans to settle in America. Dandelions, honey-bees, starlings, and kudzu, just for starters, are all imports. But none is as surprising as this one: many species of earthworms, including the redworm and the common earthworm, or nightcrawler, aren't native. They came in the soil around imported plants and in the dirt used for ballast in many ships, and they filled a very real vacuum in parts of the continent.

Until twenty thousand years ago, glaciers covered North America as far south as the Ohio River Valley. They wiped much of the slate clean, gouging out the Great Lakes and leaving a barren landscape to be recolonized as they retreated northward.

"Earthworms were probably sparse at northern latitudes following the retreat of Pleistocene glaciers," says Dr. Tim McCay, professor of biology at Colgate University. "Only a handful of native species significantly recolonized the region, leaving much of northern North America earthworm free before European colonization."

There are still regions without them. "In rural upstate New York, for example, we find no earthworms at about one-third of the forested sites that we sample," says Dr. McCay. Today, about a fourth of the earthworm species in North America are imports, although in some cases a species' status as native or exotic is presumed rather than known as fact.

In fact, says Dr. McCay, "I am amazed by the magnitude of what we do not know about earthworms in their natural settings. Of the more than two hundred species of earthworms in North America, only about a half-dozen have received much attention from scientists."

The southeastern United States, like much of unglaciated North America, is a mix of native and exotic species. A checklist of earthworms in South Carolina published in April 2014 in *Megadrilogica* and drawn from 178 sites in forty-three counties listed thirty-four species, just fourteen of which are native. Of the eleven most frequently collected, only two were native. The most common was *Amynthas diffringens,* an energetic Asian import sometimes called the "crazy worm." Others included *Dendrodrilus rubidus,* known in some quarters as the red wiggler, and *Lumbricus rubellus,* the red worm commonly sold as bait.

"The species *Dendrodrilus rubidus* provides an excellent illustration of how little we know about earthworms," says Dr. McCay. "Until 2016, we had presumed this to be a European import. Recent work by evolutionary biologists now places this species within a part of the earthworm family tree that evolved in North America. So, many biologists are now convinced that it is native."

The importance of earthworms is difficult to overstate. Aristotle called them "the intestines of the earth." Ancient Egypt banned their export. Darwin kept them in pots of dirt in his study and made them the subject of his last scientific book, saying he wanted to write about them "before joining them."

Many of us knew them first as robin food or fish bait, then as garden denizens and formaldehyde-soaked specimens in biology class. Common species range from a few to twelve inches long, are brown, red, or some combination, and are composed of more than a hundred ring-like segments. Inside is a long, marvelous digestive system perfect for turning, say, vegetable scraps into compost. From a tiny mouth, food moves through the pharynx into the esophagus, where calciferous glands essentially neutralize acid. Then it's on to a crop and a muscular gizzard that uses sand and grit in grinding up leaves, soil, and organic material. It passes through the stomach and then the intestine to the anus, emerging as nutrient-rich castings remarkably dense with substances made more usable to plants. Castings can have half again as much useful calcium, twice the carbon, three times the magnesium, five times the nitrogen, seven times the phosphorous, and eleven times the potassium as what the worm ingested, as well as increased numbers of microbes beneficial to soil and plants. The worm's own body turns much of what it eats to protein—it is 82 percent protein, compared with 3 percent for cow's milk, 40 percent for soybeans, and 50 percent for lamb.

Many earthworms tunnel incessantly as they dine, a secreted mucus helping with lubrication. Each of those ring-like segments has bristles that can serve as anchors for one section as muscles in another section expand or contract. Blood cells and hemoglobin produced by blood glands near the head flow through a network of vessels and capillaries, pumped by five heart rings wrapped around the esophagus, gizzard, and stomach. A second system of fluid-filled chambers provides firmness and structure for these boneless creatures. Direction for all this comes via cerebral ganglia that are as close to a brain as an earthworm gets.

Earthworms breathe through their skin, with oxygen and carbon dioxide passing in and out of the bloodstream. They have no eyes or nose, but the prostomium, a flap that covers the mouth, helps in sensing light and vibration.

While earthworms are transforming about a third of their weight in soil a day, they are mixing it, carrying plant material to lower levels, aerating it, and providing channels for water drainage. Moisture is a must for earthworms; direct sunlight can quickly dry them out. On the other hand, rain fills burrows with water, making it difficult for them to absorb oxygen and driving them to the surface to breathe. Their more normal emergence at night, when the ground is more likely welcomingly damp, earns them the name "nightcrawler."

There are about 7,000 species, including a six-footer found in Australia, though only about 150 are widely distributed. They have adapted to many conditions, with some nonburrowing types eating decomposing organic matter and others habituated to the seashore or the mud in streams, with only the driest deserts and polar regions completely unsuitable.

They serve as food for many species of birds; amphibians, including salamanders; insects, including beetles and termites; reptiles such as snakes, turtles, and toads; and mammals, including moles, foxes, and even bears.

They are hermaphroditic, each containing male and female sex organs. A pair of worms will exchange sperm, which travels from two male openings to two sperm receptacles. Each worm has ovaries and a clitellum, an enlarged ring visible in mature worms at about the thirtieth segment that secretes an egg case filled with protein-rich albuminous fluid. The worm in essence crawls backward out of it, with the egg case picking up eggs at the female pore and stored sperm at the male pore. The egg case then remains in the soil until the eggs emerge after two to four weeks of development, as miniaturized versions of their parents. The eggs of some species overwinter, and eggs can survive up to three years in dry soil.

While some soils contain no worms, especially rich soil can contain a million or more per acre, with moisture, pH, and the amount and quality of organic matter all factors. The biggest dangers they face these days come from humans.

"Insecticides and fungicides can reduce populations of earthworms," says Dr. McCay. Even tilling disrupts burrow systems and can reduce populations. Then there is acid rain, which, he adds, "decreases the pH of the soil and leads to decreased calcium. This negatively affects many species."

Earthworms are sold as fish bait and pet food and used for composting and gardening. They can spread plant diseases and carry parasites that can affect their predators, and they sometimes damage seedlings. When humans introduce them—often by dumping unused fishing worms, which many wildlife agencies discourage—they can disrupt new environments, particularly forests.

"Exotic earthworms can reduce the leaf-litter layer," says Dr. McCay, "which in turn reduces habitat for other animals like millipedes and salamanders, and they can reduce germination of certain plants. This is especially a problem in places that have been earthworm free since glaciation."

If you're wondering if there is room for whimsy in the world of professional worm watchers, just talk to Dr. McCay: "One of my favorite earthworms is *Amynthas hupeiensis*, a recent immigrant from Asia. This species is dark green to black, smells a bit like funky chocolate, and twists itself into knots when you pick it up."

I don't know about you, but I've got to find one.

Earthworm

Common species include *Lumbricus terrestris*, common earthworm, nightcrawler; *Lumbricus rubellus*, red earthworm; *Eisenia fetida*, composting worm.

DESCRIPTION: 3–12 inches long. Brown or reddish. Composed of more than 100 ring-like segments.
RANGE AND HABITAT: Throughout eastern U.S. except in pockets in northern New England and southern Florida.
VIEWING TIPS: Dig. A spade and a good patch of garden soil or compost should turn some up. Many emerge at night.

Red Velvet Ant

Naming animals is a provably inexact art. The koala bear isn't a bear at all; it's a marsupial. The firefly isn't a fly but a beetle. A killer whale isn't a whale, a nighthawk isn't a hawk, and the common trait that links crayfish, jellyfish, and starfish is that none are actually fish.

We all know where this is going. The red velvet ant isn't an ant; it's a wasp. The females do pretty good ant imitations, though. Three-quarters of an inch long and wingless, their black bodies tufted on the thorax and abdomen with dense orange-red hair, they look amazingly like very big ants. Differences like straight rather than elbowed antennae aren't enough to undo the deception.

But wasps they are, and, like other wasps, they can inflict repeated stings that pack enough wallop to spur their common nickname: cow killer.

"I had heard from others who had been stung by a velvet ant that 'it hurt so bad for about twenty to thirty minutes that I just wanted to die and get it over with,'" says Don Manley, professor emeritus at Clemson University. "I had worked with them for over twenty years before I was finally stung. I concur with the above description. I have not been stung by a velvet ant since—I *will not* be stung by a velvet ant again."

Red velvet ants are not normally aggressive, and if their bright coloration doesn't warn away potential predators, they can produce a squeaky chirp also designed as a warning. If escape is impossible, though, they'll prove they're all wasp. Perhaps not surprisingly, Manley, whose work with velvet ants extends back forty years, has not found a single predator for the red velvet ant.

In this species, males are rather similar to females, with the addition of black wings and the absence of a stinger. Still, says Manley, "The males have an elaborate stinging behavior that's very convincing. It can certainly make you think you're being stung. I've collected them, especially early in my career, and I've let them go at times, thinking I was being stung."

The male's wings are used in seeking out mates, with both vision and pheromones thought to play a part as they fly low over the ground in search of a female. Both sexes produce the squeak during the mating process.

Fertilized females dig through the soil and lay eggs singly on the outside of the pupa or prepupa of a ground-nesting bee or wasp. The velvet ant's exoskeleton is notoriously hard and tough enough to be resistant to the stings of the host wasp or bee.

"When the egg hatches," says Manley, "the velvet ant larva begins eating the host. Since the host is in a 'resting' stage, it has no defense." The larvae pupate inside the host nest, growing to full size in a matter of days. Some emerge in summer, while others overwinter in a pupal state.

There are approximately 150 North American species of *Dasymutilla,* the genus of velvet ants to which our red velvet ant, or *Dasymutilla occidentalis,* belongs, with most found from the desert Southwest through Mexico into Central America, and 10,000 species worldwide. Red velvet ants, found in open, sandy areas from Texas and Oklahoma through the southern states and into New England, are diurnal and are most active when the temperature is between 70 and 96 degrees.

"While the species may not be the most common," Manley says, "it is certainly the most conspicuous. When people talk about velvet ants, at least in the Southeast, that is the species to which most are referring."

This is, says Manley, "one of the later-emerging species. I usually do not see them until at least late June, sometimes early July." They remain active until September or early October, and some dig into the ground to overwinter in a quiescent state.

The adults feed largely on nectar and so can often be found in pastures and fields. It's that proximity to domestic animals that gives them their common names of cow killer and mule killer. Manley, though, has not found an instance of a red velvet ant's sting being responsible for the death of an animal of any kind. That doesn't for a minute lessen his respect for their sting. "I was being careful," he says, "and the one that stung me just barely got me. But I've worked with bees, ants and wasps my entire career, and I've been stung many times by many different things, and nothing even comes close."

He reports, reassuringly enough, that there were no lasting effects, although the knot on his thumb lasted for the better part of a month.

Nothing in the sting has diluted his appreciation for a creature that is part of a group he finds "fascinating." They're part of the natural landscape worth looking at more closely—although with the respect their formidable defensive abilities merit.

Red Velvet Ant

DESCRIPTION: Three-quarters of an inch long; black with tufts of red/orange hair. Large and solitary.
RANGE AND HABITAT: Sandy open soils; fields, fence rows, pastures; much of the Southeast.
VIEWING TIPS: Sandy soils, particularly fields and pastures, can be especially promising.

Coyote

In one of the best-ever episodes of *The Simpsons,* Homer eats hot chili peppers that trigger a series of hallucinations. In a bizarre desert world, he arrives at a pyramid where he meets his spirit guide in the form of a coyote, voiced by Johnny Cash.

The notion that a coyote could bridge the temporal and spirit worlds would not have seemed outlandish to any number of Native American peoples. Coyotes—cunning, intelligent, indefatigable—play major roles in the belief systems of many of the tribes of the Plains and the Southwest. In Navajo tales the coyote is a trickster, a wise counselor, even a deity.

"Coyote is one of the major players in creation, in the making of the constellations," says Delores Noble, an indigenous language and culture consultant from Steamboat, Arizona, and former senior education specialist with the Navajo Office of Diné Culture and Language. "In fact, we have a series of coyote stories told through the winter to our students. They are moral stories that help them to become thinkers and help instill in them wisdom."

European settlers had their own tales and imbued the coyote with similar mystical powers. One legend held that the coyote could hypnotize a chicken on a roost and get it to fall, mesmerized, into its gaping jaws.

We have a primal connection to the handful of canid species in the world—wolves, jackals, foxes, dingoes—recognizing in them some of our own best and worst attributes. In their cleverness and playfulness, their cunning and ruthlessness, in both their solitary and communal guises, we see ourselves. Of all the relationships we have with the animals we have domesticated, our link with dogs is perhaps the most intimate and the most mystical.

Coyotes are wily opportunists, and it is when they compete with us or steal from us that we most loathe them and are the most brutal in our reprisals. Known to poach our livestock, they have been killed by the tens of thousands, and yet they have steadily extended their range and numbers. In the eastern United States, coyotes are relative newcomers, moving into an ecological niche once occupied by wolves. Native to the western United States, they came east in two waves—across southern Canada and through Louisiana and Arkansas, gaining ascendance in the Southeast since the 1970s. In some southeastern states, they had human help.

"They were often introduced by fox hunters who released them into large enclosures called fox pens for running with hounds," says Dr. John Kilgo, a research wildlife biologist with the U.S. Forest Service. "Inevitably, some escaped."

These adaptable animals are found in every type of southeastern habitat, from the mountains to the coastal swamps. After years of expansion, though, Kilgo says, "Data that goes back ten to fifteen years indicate a leveling of their numbers, or at least not a continued increase."

Like many animals, coyotes vary in size by latitude. In the Southeast, they are a little smaller than German shepherds, which they resemble to some degree, with pointed, erect ears, a long, thin muzzle, and a drooping tail. Their color can range from light blond to black (or melanistic), and the Southeast has more melanistic coyotes than other regions—10 to 20 percent of the population, "almost invariably with a white patch on their chest," according to Kilgo. They can weigh anywhere from twenty to seventy-five pounds across their range, although in the Southeast they generally weigh between twenty-five and thirty-five pounds. They are fast, capable of hitting forty miles per hour, and have great stamina, stalking or traveling over long distances.

And they are omnivores. "The most common thread among the half-dozen or so diet studies published in the Southeast is the variability in the diet," says Kilgo. "I would rank deer and small mammals, including rabbits and rodents, about equally at the top, with insects, carrion, berries, and fruits all part of their diet. Berries and fruits are often the number one food item during the seasons they're available, basically May through October."

They will kill livestock and are thought to take up to 1 percent of the nation's domestic sheep. They have also been known to kill dogs and cats, although such reports are not numerous. While they are basically solitary hunters, they will gather in pairs or packs to take down adult deer, although not in numbers sufficient to affect the population.

Fawns are another matter. "Ample research in the Southeast, including ours at the Savannah River Site," says Kilgo, "shows that they can have a huge effect on deer populations just by the numbers of fawns they take. The reproductive success of deer in many areas can be severely limited, meaning hunters in those areas can't shoot as many does as they used to or the deer population will decline further. The bottom line is that coyotes have changed the way we manage deer, and many states have begun to limit numbers of deer tags issued to compensate for the effects of predation on fawns."

Coyotes breed from January through March in the Southeast, forming monogamous pairs. Though they generally bed down in tall grass and brush, they will dig new burrows or expand those of other animals to raise their young and may use abandoned barns or outbuildings. Gestation lasts just over two months, and a litter can contain well over a dozen pups, although five to seven is average. There have been reports of coy-dogs, crossbreeds between dogs and coyotes, but this seems to be a relatively rare phenomenon.

Both adults hunt and regurgitate food for the young, which stay in the den for most of the first month and are weaned at about two months. Young males leave the family group late in the fall, while females may remain into the next spring. As with most animals, survival rates are low, and sometimes only one or two members of a litter will make it to adulthood.

Coyotes have a loose pack structure, with the breeding pair as alphas, sometimes accompanied by offspring from previous litters known as betas. "Then there are transients," says Kilgo, "usually, but not always, young dispersers that are more or less nomadic until they find a territory to settle in. Those generally are not tolerated."

The upshot, though, is that "only a small portion—20 percent or less—of the total population in an area may breed in any given year."

Coyotes, which host fleas, ticks, worms, and other parasites, are also susceptible to a variety of diseases, including distemper, mange, hepatitis, and West Nile virus.

"Very little is known about disease effects on populations," says Kilgo, as few coyotes are tested. "Mortality from disease seems to be fairly low among adults, though some die of heartworm infections, and parvo probably takes its toll on pups. There are no confirmed cases of distemper causing illness or death, but we did test twenty-three individuals for distemper (among other diseases) and found four to be positive. The rabies variant we have in the Southeast is most common in raccoons, foxes, and bats. Coyotes are indeed susceptible, as is any mammal, but it is pretty rare in coyotes in the Southeast. It is most common in coyotes in south Texas."

Although they are a relatively new addition to the southeastern landscape, coyotes hearken back to a time when wolves populated the region, renewing our often-ambivalent relationship with the family of wild creatures whose descendants are now with us as pets. Now, as then, it's hard to escape the sense that the kinship with these intelligent creatures is more than physical.

Coyote

DESCRIPTION: Often like a small German shepherd with erect ears, slim muzzle, and bushy tail held downward, with color ranging from light blond to black. Height 2 feet tall at shoulder, generally 25–35 pounds.
RANGE AND HABITAT: Versatile; can adapt to many climates. Found through most of North and Central America and throughout the Southeast.
VIEWING TIPS: Generally nocturnal. Late evenings and early mornings are good viewing times.

PART III

Water

Bullfrog

If the "bull" that kicks off the word "bullfrog" strikes you as hyperbole, think again. To many of the creatures that call the average pond home, the bullfrog more than merits the appellation. For them, it is, in fact, the stuff of horror movies.

In the spring, it crawls up out of the muck on the bottom, huge and hungry. Its booming call can be heard for half a mile on a calm evening, earning the comparison with its burly namesake.

Its appetite is undiscriminating—it will eat virtually anything that fits into its gaping mouth. And until it does, it sits, fat and sloe-eyed as Jabba the Hutt, waiting for its next meal to come along. Even other bullfrogs had best watch out. A male bullfrog will defend several yards of shoreline, and if that bellow doesn't work, it will resort to a clumsy but ferocious form of sumo wrestling, splashing about and grappling other males with its short forearms.

The bullfrog lords it over much of local aquatic life, eating all manner of insects, worms, and spiders, as well as other frogs, fish, small snakes and turtles, lizards, salamanders, crawfish, shrews, moles, birds, and—on at least one reported occasion—a bat.

Fortunately, they do not go unchecked where they are native, as in the Southeast, where they are simply a part of a balanced ecosystem. Their own predators can include water snakes, snapping turtles, herons, opossums, skunks, raccoons, and predatory fish such as bass and gar.

But where bullfrogs have been introduced—often in unsuccessful attempts to raise them for restaurants, as in much of the American West, some of the Caribbean islands, and parts of Europe, Asia, and South America—they do not face such predation and have long since worn out their welcome, dining voraciously on most everything that happens by, virtually unscathed by predators.

"Through their use as food (frog legs), the pet trade, and medical research, and facilitated by their tolerance for habitats degraded by human activities, bullfrogs have been introduced and are thriving around the world," says Dr. J. D. Willson, associate professor of biology at the University of Arkansas. "In the western U.S., their populations have exploded, and they are partially to blame for drastic reductions in the numbers of many native frogs, such as the endangered Chiricahua leopard frog and the foothills yellow-legged frog. In addition to directly eating these smaller frogs, bullfrogs have played a role in spreading diseases that threaten amphibians worldwide."

Most of us encounter bullfrogs more often by sound than by sight, and it is quite a sound—the bass-rich and resonant note, transcribed as "jug-o-rum," is made by a vocal pouch under the lower jaw. We sometimes spy them hanging limp in the water, just the tips of their snouts and their bulbous, golden eyes visible. They often hide amid vegetation or under overhanging banks during the day, calling and dining at night. Normally from three to six inches in length, they have been known to reach eight inches, with ten-inch legs, and to weigh more than a pound. They are brown or green, with undersides that are white to yellow. The males' throats tend toward yellow, particularly during the breeding season, when their forelegs swell and the bases of their thumbs get larger.

Both sexes have large ear membranes behind and below the eyes, with the male's about twice the size of the eye and the female's somewhat smaller. Their long, muscular legs end in webbed feet, which are great for swimming, and their shorter front legs act as shock absorbers when they land after jumping. As with many other amphibians, their skin is gas-permeable, enabling them at times to breathe underwater.

Bullfrogs begin breeding as soon as it is relatively warm, usually in April or May. Adults gather in breeding ponds, where males stake out territories, bellowing to attract females and warn off other males. The male grasps a receptive female and fertilizes the eggs as she lays them. The eggs, small, clear bubbles with dark nuclei, spread in a thin, gelatinous sheet across the water's surface. In four to five days, the eggs become little tadpoles, which wriggle free of the egg sacs. Those tadpoles, with both gills and tails, grow for one to two years (as much as three years in some cold northern locations), eating algae and plant tissue, prey to everything from water bugs to fish and other frogs. Mature tadpoles are among the largest of those of any frogs, commonly more than six inches in length, and are able to coexist with predatory fish. Toward the end of the larval period, there is a final amazing transformation.

"Over the course of a few weeks," says Willson, "a bullfrog goes from a swimming vegetarian to an air-breathing, terrestrial predator—requiring the growth of legs and lungs, the loss of gills, fins, and tail, and a complete restructuring of the digestive, immune, and feeding systems." They may take an additional two or more years to reach breeding age.

"The reproductive potential of bullfrogs is amazing," adds Willson. "A single female can lay more than twenty-thousand eggs in one breeding event, eggs that hatch and grow into tadpoles too large to be prey for most fish and other aquatic predators. It is not uncommon to walk to the edge of a pond in summer and see swarms of bullfrog tadpoles rippling the shallow water and hundreds of newly metamorphosed young frogs scattering in all directions along the shoreline."

Both tadpoles and adults will hibernate in cold weather, burying themselves in mud. During warmer winters, they may just reduce their activity level. They can tolerate higher water temperatures than many other species, something that allows for longer reproductive seasons and higher survival rates. It also allows them to thrive longer in environments that have been affected by human activities.

Besides being used for food—frog legs most likely came from a bullfrog —they are used in research, since their musculoskeletal, digestive, and nervous systems are similar to those of many other animals, including humans.

As wildlife watchers, we can of course appreciate them just as much in their natural setting, where they live, on average, four to five years, bringing to summer nights that powerful voice and reigning as lords of the pond.

Bullfrog

DESCRIPTION: 3–8 inches long, 10-inch legs; green/brown, with light undersides.

RANGE AND HABITAT: Native to eastern United State. Introduced in West. Throughout Southeast except southern Florida, where they are replaced by the similar pig frog.

VIEWING TIPS: Listen for that booming call near ponds, swamps, wetlands. Often hide amid vegetation or under overhanging banks.

Shrimp

In the natural world, the wondrous isn't hard to come by. Owls fly noiselessly. Flies can land upside down. Many snakes can unhinge their jaws. Look deeper and tinker a little, and things get even better. An enzyme in the stomachs of calves makes cheese possible. Compounds taken from fireflies were used to test for life on Mars.

And then there is chitosan. This remarkable compound is derived from a natural substance that is tossed into trash bags and washed down garbage disposals by the ton—in the shells of shrimp and some other crustaceans. It's "bioadhesive," so it sticks to damp human tissue and helps clot blood. It also has natural antibacterial properties, so it's perfect for bandages, and it's used for that purpose on the battlefield. In other settings, it enhances plant growth, helps defend against fungal infections, and can help purify water, wine, and beer.

Outside the human purview, chitosan, a form of chitin, plays a key role in molting, something shrimp do pretty regularly—well over a dozen times. Chitin takes the stage after a shrimp sheds its exoskeleton, becoming a framework for the fusion of calcium carbonate, which is omnipresent in seawater and responsible for forming the shrimp's new, larger outer shell.

But let's go back to the beginning.

For brown and pink shrimp, two of the three species with substantial commercial value in the Atlantic and the Gulf of Mexico, reproduction begins when the male shrimp transfers a spermatophore, a capsule-like container of sperm, to the molted, soft-shelled female, who stores it until she is ready to spawn. The third species, white shrimp, mates between molts when the shell is still hard, with the male attaching a sperm packet to the female's underside.

Females then lay half a million to one million eggs each in offshore waters, with different species preferring different depths.

"Shrimp engage in batch spawning," says Peyton Cagle, fisheries biologist with the Louisiana Department of Wildlife and Fisheries, "meaning they can spawn multiple times in a season. This is what makes the species so prolific."

Within a day, each egg, just one sixty-fourth of an inch across, has hatched and the larval shrimp, or nauplius, feeds on yolk reserves. The nauplius is essentially just another speck of plankton at this point, and the growing shrimp remains in this form for four more stages.

The shrimp undergoes three stages as a protozoan, in which it develops mouth parts and an abdomen, begins feeding on algae, and reaches about one-twelfth of an inch in length. Three mysid stages grow the shrimp to a fifth of an inch in length and give it the beginnings of legs and antennae; then two postlarval stages take the white and pink to about a quarter of an inch and the brown, which appears to stay offshore longer, to about four-tenths of an inch, with both having developed walking and swimming legs and the general appearance of an adult. Full development takes several weeks and moves the shrimp from the sea bottom to the brackish water at the mouth of a stream or river.

"The juvenile to subadult phase," says Cagle, "is where you see the most rapid growth. As juveniles grow into subadults, you see the migration from marsh edges into more open bays. Many subadult shrimp are harvested during inshore shrimp seasons. Then, growth slows as it enters the subadult and adult phases."

"Pink shrimp," adds David Whitaker of the South Atlantic Fishery Management Council, "require sandy bottoms as juveniles, compared to whites and browns, which do well on muddy bottoms. Thus, browns and whites are found mostly where relatively large rivers bring sediments to the estuaries."

The shrimp's body is divided into three segments—head, thorax, and abdomen. The head and thorax are fused together and covered by a carapace that encloses the gills and comes to a point called the rostrum. The head has eyes on stalks and at least two pairs of long antennae—eight to ten inches for browns and pinks and up to twenty inches for whites, two or three times longer than their bodies (the largest white shrimp recorded was ten inches long, not counting antennae). There are fourteen pairs of appendages—the first three, near the head, are modified into mouth parts called maxillipeds; the next five are walking legs attached to the thorax; there are five pairs of swimming legs on the abdomen and one pair forming part of the fan-like tail. The ten pairs of walking and swimming legs justify the name decapod, which includes crabs and lobsters.

Most human appreciation of the shrimp is, of course, culinary. We're drawn to the shrimp's muscular body, which, boiled or pan fried with butter and garlic, provides one of the most exquisite human dining experiences. There are two thousand species of shrimp in the world, with hundreds harvested from fresh and saltwater, and those three with the most commercial value here. Brown shrimp are found along the Atlantic and Gulf coasts, most plentifully in summer months, spawning in relatively deep water in the fall. White shrimp are found in the Atlantic as far south as central Florida and in the Gulf from the panhandle of Florida to southern Texas and on to Mexico. They are more plentiful in the early spring and late fall when water is cooler, with the spring catch composed of large spawning adults and the fall catch made up of the offspring, which get gradually larger over the fall. Pink shrimp are mainly landed off the Florida coast and are more available in colder weather, from fall until early spring.

The U.S. commercial shrimping industry has fallen on extremely hard times recently.

"There are multiple factors," says Amber Von Harten, a fisheries specialist formerly with the South Carolina Sea Grant Extension Program, "the first being the flood of imports of pond-raised shrimp hitting U.S. markets, driving prices down to what shrimpers were getting in the 1960s."

"Working inflation and fuel prices into the computation," adds Whitaker, "would show an even worse scenario for fishermen. Taken together, these factors have resulted in significant changes in fishing behavior—shrimpers fishing only when catches are expected to be good."

There are, he says, "virtually no wooden traditional Florida-built wooden trawlers being built, and the ones that remain active are at least forty years old. In the Atlantic, some are shifting to smaller, more fuel-efficient boats, and others are moving to large steel-hull boats with onboard freezers, staying out longer and traveling more widely, working only the areas where shrimp are abundant. In one recent week, Charleston's primary shrimp port, Shem Creek, had only ten trawlers, where it used to have between forty and sixty. We may see an eventual shift to passive gears like traps or nets fishing the ebb tides. Personally, I hope the trawlers can continue to be common sites in the waters off the coast and remain cultural icons."

Overall, says Whitaker, "I expect fuel prices will ultimately rise again and put more pressure on shrimp trawlers. Imports are not likely to decline, although we have observed periodic disease problems in Asian shrimp farms, which caused shrimp prices for domestic fishermen to go up for a while."

All of that is reflected in harvest figures. The combined Atlantic and Gulf landings of shrimp in 2017 for all species, according to the National Marine Fisheries Service, was 239 million pounds, down from more than 300 million pounds in 2000, with both figures dwarfed by imports of 1.5 billion pounds.

In recent years, states and the federal government have tightened restrictions on imported seafood, with Congress mandating that shrimp imported beginning in 2019 be accompanied by harvest and landing data as well as chain-of-custody records. In fighting what it calls the importation of "illegal, unreported, and unregulated" seafood, it says that such practices "jeopardize the health of fish stocks, distort legal markets . . . and unfairly compete with the products of law-abiding fishermen, aquaculture producers and seafood producers." In the spring of 2019, Louisiana began requiring restaurants to list the country of origin for shrimp and crawfish.

Shrimp are prolific breeders, and, given the dramatic decline in the number of shrimpers, their population can be expected to continue to do well, barring adverse environmental conditions. Meanwhile, a dramatic increase in shrimping worldwide, mostly in the form of shrimp farming, has had dramatic environmental and economic effects, and there are no doubt battles and challenges remaining.

In the meantime, it's worth remembering as wildlife watchers that this widely exploited species is notable for its natural history and its wondrous role in one corner of the world of science.

White Shrimp, *Litopenaeus setiferus;* Brown Shrimp, *Farfantepanaeus aztecus;* Pink Shrimp, *Farfantepanaeus duorarum*

DESCRIPTION: Shrimp range from a fraction of an inch to 9 inches in length, with exoskeletons in 3 parts, antennae, and 14 pairs of appendages.
RANGE AND HABITAT: Species inhabit many of the world's ocean waters. They can be found along most of the Atlantic and Gulf coasts, with good concentrations in some pockets.
VIEWING TIPS: Estuaries and near-shore waters. Often caught as bait and observed jumping in boat wakes in shallow waters.

Loggerhead Sea Turtle

There are two moments in a loggerhead sea turtle's life when it is, shall we say, anthropomorphically gifted. The first comes just after its hatching, as it scrambles up out of the nest and across a short stretch of beach. Part of the scene's emotional resonance lies in the fact that the dash, undertaken with a frantic and vulnerable squadron of siblings, ends not in guaranteed safety but in an ocean offering an apprenticeship as a paddling hors d'oeuvre. In fact, it's estimated that only one out of a thousand hatchlings will make it to adulthood.

The second is when those females who have survived the ocean's perils for thirty years or so return to the beach to reproduce. On a spring or summer night, one will lumber from the sea, looking every bit like the pre-Jurassic throwback she is, and move to the base of a dune above the high-tide line. There, flailing with all four flippers, she will dig a shallow body pit and settle into it. Using her rear flippers as scoops, she will dig a chamber shaped like a large inverted light bulb and fill it with eggs during twenty strenuous minutes of laying.

Through this, she will sigh on occasion, blinking away freely flowing tears (actually excretions from a gland that removes salt from her system) and raising and lowering her head and back flippers with the effort of depositing each small group of eggs. It looks for all the world like a selfless, sorrowful, and exhausting effort on behalf of the ten-dozen leathery, ping-pong-ball-size eggs she will leave behind. She then fills in the egg chamber and tamps down the sand with her plastron, or lower shell. With some additional swipes of her front flippers, she flings more sand in an attempt to disguise the true location. The entire process takes more than an hour.

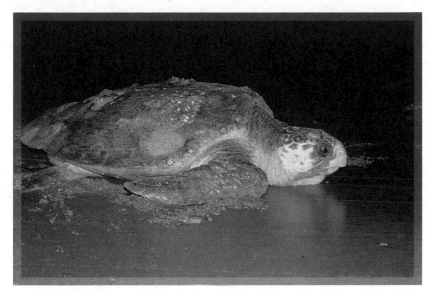

She repeats this process four or five times, approximately every two weeks during the nesting season, normally May through August, with eggs fertilized about a month before her first onshore trek as she mated with one or perhaps several males along her migratory route. Those eggs will produce predominantly male hatchlings if incubation temperatures remain below 84 degrees and primarily female if above.

"Once she returns to the sea," says Sally Murphy, a biologist retired from the South Carolina Department of Natural Resources (SCDNR) and the author of *Turning the Tide: A Memoir* (Evening Post Books, 2019), "she will find a protected spot, perhaps near a reef or shoal, to rest and begin producing the next clutch of eggs. Because of her rigid shell, she does not feed during the nesting season, since there is not enough room for a full stomach and the several hundred eggs being produced."

Generally, the only time people ever see loggerheads is during one of these two episodes, which take place in many locations along the Atlantic seaboard, from North Carolina to Florida and in a few spots in the Gulf, south to the Yucatan. That is why, says Murphy, who has studied logger-heads since 1976 and who was coleader of the first Marine Turtle Recovery Team in the nation, so many people get emotionally involved with them and become so protective. It's one reason thousands of residents in coastal states spend time and energy working to protect the nests laid on their beaches each summer.

Volunteers walk or ride ATVs at dawn over most of the coast, looking for the telltale tracks that let them know a nesting female has been there. They move eggs to better locations when necessary or cover nests with plastic mesh to protect them from predators. They pick up trash, fill in deep holes dug by beachgoers, and transport sick or injured turtles for treatment. They also answer phones, give lectures, and work to get the word out on various conservation measures such as reducing beach lighting, which can confuse mothers and hatchlings.

In the late 1970s, when the loggerhead was first listed as threatened by the federal government, populations throughout the Southeast were in steep decline, to a great extent because of shrimp nets, in which turtles were caught and drowned. In the summer of 1980, a volunteer stranding network recorded nearly six hundred dead sea turtles in South Carolina and eight hundred in Georgia. A congressionally mandated analysis by the National Research Council found that shrimp trawls accounted for more sea turtle deaths than all other factors combined.

The legal fight to get turtle excluder devices (TEDs) into shrimp trawls lasted decades and ended up in many state and federal courtrooms. In 1988, South Carolina was the first state to require the use of TEDs, which allow turtles to escape the shrimp nets. Florida did likewise in 1989, and Georgia followed suit in 1991.

One of the volunteer nest protection groups, led by Chris Marlow and Jeff McClary, a plumber and an electrician, respectively, was called South Carolina United Turtle Enthusiasts (SCUTE). They were the first in South Carolina to tackle the problem of disorientation of hatchlings caused by beachside lighting. Their effort began with better protection of turtle nests on Pawleys Island and expanded its reach along much of the state's northern coastline. They drew on research on how and why light affects sea turtles, much of it conducted in Florida.

"They convinced Georgetown County Council to pass a lighting ordi-nance," says Murphy, "worked with Santee Cooper [an electric utility com-pany] to get streetlights shaded, and produced a bumper sticker that said,

'Sea turtles dig the dark,' and a catchy public service announcement for TV." The U.S. Fish and Wildlife Service produced large blue signs with a hatchling that said, "Lights Out," for all states to post at access points to beach towns and communities.

The effort to save loggerheads includes management, research, education —and monitoring, as it's important to determine population trends over time. Murphy's husband, Tom, also with the SCDNR, has done radio telemetry, attaching tracking devices to female turtles, and found that they spend the two weeks between nestings within five miles of the coast, which is the main shrimping grounds. In the late 1990s and early 2000s, Sally Murphy and others in Georgia and North Carolina used satellite telemetry to find out where loggerheads go after the nesting season and found that they inhabit an area stretching from New Jersey to the Florida Keys and the Bahamas.

Their research has shown that loggerheads lead a wide-ranging existence.

"They leave here as two-inch hatchlings and get caught up in the Atlantic gyre currents," Sally Murphy says. "By the time they're a foot long, they're in the Azores, off Africa, and in the western Mediterranean, and might remain there for ten to fifteen years or so. As they grow, they can no longer find ample food in their oceanic environments. When they return to feeding grounds on the Continental Shelf of the Southeast United States, they're eighteen or twenty inches long and eating various crab and mollusk species, using their strong jaws to crack through shells. Juvenile loggerheads from North and South Carolina and Georgia mix with Florida and Mexican turtles on the feeding grounds. When it comes time to nest for the first time at thirty years of age, they return to the region where they were hatched.

"The five different nesting groups—Northern, Florida Peninsula, Northern Gulf of Mexico, Dry Tortugas, and Greater Caribbean—are genetically distinct subpopulations," Murphy adds, "so if we lose ours, they will not be replaced by Florida or Mexican turtles."

Fortunately, there is good news, at least in the short term, according to Dennis Klemm, Sea Turtle Recovery Coordinator for the Southeast Regional Office, National Marine Fisheries Service: "The Northern Recovery Unit (from southern Virginia to the Georgia/Florida border) is actually shattering some of the records kept since they've been doing nesting beach surveys. That unit's looking really good right now. Of course, while one big year is always great, what really matters are long-term trends."

"The Florida Peninsula Recovery Unit (entire eastern coast, west coast to a little north of Tampa Bay) is the largest recovery unit by far, representing one of the biggest nesting aggregations in the world for loggerheads," Klemm continues. "The number of nests is increasing at this time, but because of a down period in the early to mid-2000s, when there was a lot of concern about nesting, we can't yet say the increases we see are a long-term trend. In the short term, though, they are increasing."

Klemm goes on: "The Northern Gulf of Mexico Recovery Unit (from Franklin County on the Florida Panhandle through Texas), with up to a few thousand nests per year, and the Dry Tortugas (islands west of Key West) Recovery Unit, with a few hundred nests per year, are both small recovery units. They both appear to be stable overall, but due to the small size, variability is more pronounced.

"There is one other Loggerhead Recovery Unit, the Greater Caribbean, covering nesting beaches from Mexico through French Guiana, the Bahamas, and Lesser and Greater Antilles. The population typically sees nests numbering in the thousands annually, but good trend data is not available at this time."

Overall, the National Oceanographic and Atmospheric Administration estimates there are approximately sixty-eight thousand to ninety thousand nests in the United States per year, on about ninety nesting beaches between North Carolina and Mississippi. South Florida's concentration is the highest, with more than ten thousand females nesting per year.

Overall numbers are one thing. For Murphy, sometimes it's personal; she has been particularly delighted by one family tree. She says, "Genetic studies by the University of Georgia, using DNA fingerprinting techniques, have discovered a female nesting on Cape Island in Cape Romain National Wildlife Refuge, along with nine of her daughters. Three more of her daughters and two granddaughters are nesting in Georgia. The grandmother is at least ninety years old!"

Still, a strong rebound sustained for a substantial period of time would be necessary to change the loggerhead's threatened status. And turtles face other obstacles. In fact, all seven species of sea turtles are either endangered or threatened. What seems certain now is that the volunteer nesting protection projects begun in the early 1980s and the use of TEDs have been effective. It is also clear that given reproductive maturity at thirty years, there is no quick fix.

"Loggerheads, managers, and volunteers," says Murphy, "all need to have staying power."

Loggerhead Sea Turtle

DESCRIPTION: Adults have a shell about 31–43 inches long and can weigh 200–300 pounds. The upper parts of the body are a dark mahogany brown, with yellow on the underside.

RANGE AND HABITAT: Found in most of the world's oceans but nest in the more temperate regions near the tropics of Capricorn and Cancer. Come ashore to lay eggs. Nesting sites are from North Carolina to south Florida and along the Gulf coast to the Yucatan.

VIEWING TIPS: As loggerheads are threatened, a guided nature program is best for you and for them.

Bottlenose Dolphin

Imagine, for a moment, the plight of the bottlenose dolphin mother. Born after a year's gestation, her calf measures three feet long, weighs forty pounds or so, and quickly becomes playful and inquisitive. The trouble, of course, is that the youngster can roam in three dimensions, and the neighborhood may well include large, hungry sharks. Constant vigilance on the mother's part is, at the very least, a good idea. If Junior gets careless in the face of danger, she may slap the water with her tail, shove him toward the surface with her blunt beak, or simply push him to the bottom and hold him there—in effect, enforcing an underwater "time out" until he gets the message to cool it.

Dolphin young may nurse, by the way, anywhere from two to more than four years, but the animals have developed their own system of day care to allow the mother a chance to wander off and feed now and then. Creating what amounts to a spherical playpen, a number of females will sometimes gather around a baby, forming a living barrier between it and danger.

The socialization implied in all that is a day-to-day fact of dolphin life, for dolphins live in fluid groups that may have from ten to a hundred members.

"Inshore groups tend to be fairly small," says Dr. Randall Wells, director of the Sarasota Dolphin Research Program. "Group composition changes frequently in this fission/fusion society, unlike the stable 'pods' in which some dolphin species such as killer whales live. The groups consist of mothers and calves, juvenile males and females independent of their mothers, or adult males, sometimes in strongly bonded alliance pairs."

Within these groups, dolphins have been known to stay with sick or injured fellows and nudge them to the surface until they can swim on their own. That, of course, is important because the dolphin is a mammal, requiring atmospheric oxygen—obtained through a whale-like blowhole—for breathing. Dolphins have also been known to hold the occasional human afloat in a similar manner.

Still, dolphins, like most other animals, have never fared very well at the hands of humans. On the East Coast, entanglement in gillnets and crab trap float lines, recreational fishing gear entanglement, hooking, ingestion, loss of habitat, boat strikes, and pollution are all hazards. There are natural dangers as well. In the late 1980s, more than half of the coastal migratory stock of bottlenose dolphins off the Atlantic coast died from a viral infection related to measles and canine distemper.

"A recurrence in 2013–15 along the Atlantic seaboard," says Wells, "resulted in the deaths of about 1,650 more bottlenose dolphins."

The bottlenose dolphin is our "Flipper," the common, social species people most often see from their docks or below coastal bridges in the Southeast. Dolphins will frequently ride on the bow pressure waves of ships moving at speeds up to twenty-five miles per hour, surfing and performing leaping acrobatics. They power their swimming with their horizontal tail flukes, using their dorsal fins—which sometimes get them mistaken for sharks—for balance and steering. Sally Murphy, a biologist retired from the Wildlife Diversity Section of the South Carolina Department of Natural Resources, says these dorsal fins often develop distinctive notches from injury, such as those caused by predators including great white, bull, and tiger sharks. "These are used by researchers to identify individuals. Wildlife watchers can also look for these unusual fins to recognize 'regulars' in their area of the coast."

Individuals can be twelve feet long and weigh seven hundred pounds. The animals have very large brains, thought to have evolved in large measure to process all the acoustic information that goes into being a dolphin, as they communicate through a wide range of sounds and, like bats, use echolocation to find and identify objects.

The bottlenose takes its name from its blunt, truncated beak, which is filled, by the way, with up to ninety very sharp teeth, used to grasp prey fish that dolphins typically swallow whole. An individual can eat more than twenty pounds of fish a day, and they are also known to eat squid, shrimp, cuttlefish, and mollusks.

Dolphins may feed singly or band together, engaging in coordinated group fishing. A group will surround a school of fish, then rush in to pick off and eat individuals. They have also been known to chase fish completely out of the water, then beach themselves, eat, and return to the water, an activity called strand-feeding. "In South Carolina it occurs day or night and usually two hours before or after low tide," says Murphy. "Dolphins also 'play' with their food—one was observed near Hilton Head Island using a flounder like a frisbee."

Realizing that our own fishing has threatened dolphins, humans have slowly begun to try to make the practice less destructive. In 1972 the U.S. Marine Mammal Protection Act made it illegal, with a few exceptions, to kill or capture marine mammals in U.S. waters or to import them, and in 1989 the U.N. General Assembly limited the use of drift nets, which capture whatever swims into them and can stretch for fifty miles.

Though their numbers are not what they once were, Wells says, "While the status of bottlenose dolphins varies from population to population around the world, globally, as a species, they are not endangered."

Females reproduce every two to six years, with females reaching sexual maturity between the ages of five and twelve, and males between ten and thirteen. Males compete for access to females and both sexes take multiple mates. Gestation lasts about a year and single births are the norm, although twins are possible.

It's not hard for us to relate to the intelligence and perceived playfulness of the bottlenose dolphin. We recognize our kinship with them, something any dedicated wildlife watcher will want to do with an ever-expanding list of species. In this case, it's worth hoping that increased awareness and regulations will help this impressive creature flourish.

Bottlenose Dolphin

DESCRIPTION: Length up to 12.5 feet, weight up to 600–700 pounds, though typically smaller in coastal waters. Dark gray on back, lighter on flanks and belly.

RANGE AND HABITAT: Warm and warm temperate waters worldwide. Throughout the Atlantic and the Gulf of Mexico. Primarily coastal, but some are found over continental shelfs and in deep offshore waters.

VIEWING TIPS: Watch for their dorsal fins and undulating swimming and for their jumping.

Atlantic Horseshoe Crab

I'm one of those people who hopes we make contact with an alien civilization or two. I wonder about the possibilities when it comes to extraterrestrial life and who among our scientists and science fiction writers has been on the right track.

Fortunately, I am also one of those people awestruck by the variations played out right here on earth. I've been writing species profiles for more than a quarter of a century, and I have yet to run across a creature, no matter how common, that didn't offer something wondrous upon the least real reflection.

Some offer special riches, with fireflies, hummingbirds, skunks, sea cucumbers, and electric eels among the more compellingly exotic. Then there is the horseshoe crab, which may well give us a mild foretaste of the wonders that lie beyond this lovely but troubled little planet. It is a remarkable assemblage of features, a testament to the variety possible among living organisms and to their potential stability as well.

First, the variety. Like Mr. Spock, the horseshoe crab has blood whose oxidizing agent is copper-based hemocyanin rather than the iron-based hemoglobin, so it bleeds dark blue/green. Its blood also contains a substance used to test for bacterial contamination, making it valuable enough to the pharmaceutical industry—it can bring $15,000 per quart—that it is harvested and then released again after about a third of that blood is removed.

The horseshoe crab has nine eyes, two of them complex and the rest simple, on its large helmet-like head or prosoma, including two on its underside, and a tenth that consists of rudimentary light receptors spread along its tail. Those eyes were the subject of part of the research work on physiological and chemical processes related to vision that earned the 1967 Nobel Prize in medicine.

There is much more: The horseshoe crab's brain and heart lie within that prosoma, which is greenish-gray to brown and shaped somewhat like a horseshoe, and its gaping, jawless mouth is set amid the legs on its underside; its long tail, which acts as a rudder, is strong enough that the crab can use it to right itself should it be flipped onto its back; and, like a small and fortunate number of creatures, it can regrow limbs.

The stability of that unusual design is impressive. Horseshoe crabs date to the Ordovician period, roughly 450 million years ago, and are, in that sense, living fossils, little changed since well before the dinosaurs.

Limulus polyphemus is one of four species of horseshoe crabs, the only one in the Western Hemisphere. While it can be found from Maine to southern Mexico, it is most abundant in an area centered on the Delaware Bay and stretching from Virginia to New Jersey. There are six subspecies—Gulf of Maine, Mid-Atlantic, Southeast, Florida Atlantic, Northeast Gulf of Mexico, and Yucatan Peninsula.

When it comes to the Gulf population, Dr. Elizabeth Wenner, a marine scientist retired from the South Carolina Department of Natural Resources, says, "Horseshoe crabs breed in all coastal counties along the west coast of Florida. Farther west, horseshoe crabs are rarer along the coasts of Alabama and Mississippi. They are rare in Louisiana and are not known to exist currently in Texas."

The horseshoe crab is not a true crab at all. It is more closely related to spiders and scorpions, ticks and mites. It lives in the sand and mud of the ocean bottom, where it burrows for worms and mollusks, spending winters along the continental shelf, then moving in late spring to shallow coastal waters to reproduce, with males arriving first and waiting for the much larger females.

"The timing is pretty critical," says Dr. Wenner. "Water temperature and beach composition are both important, and much of the mating happens from March to May, during nightly spring tides, at full moon."

A male uses glove-like claws on one pair of legs to grasp a female's shell, and the female pulls him along as she leaves the water, digs a series of five to seven small holes, and deposits from three to four thousand green eggs one-sixteenth of an inch long in each of them. A female may lay anywhere from sixty thousand to one hundred thousand eggs in one season. The male fertilizes them as he is pulled along, and, since males greatly outnumber females, multiple males often fertilize one female's eggs.

"One of the most amazing things I've ever witnessed," says Dr. Wenner, "is thousands of horseshoe crabs in the water on a spawning beach. There was a frenzy of activity, with many satellite males forming a daisy chain, connected one to another to another, with one male latched onto the female. The power of those pheromones to draw them ashore at that particular time when all the conditions were right was awesome."

Shorebirds, especially red knots, which stop during their twelve-thousand-mile migration from Tierra del Fuego to the Arctic, gorge themselves on those eggs, often doubling their weight. In fact, reductions in the number of horseshoe crabs have had major impacts on the numbers of red knots and other birds.

"It brings up what a great web of interconnection we're part of," says Dr. Wenner, "how a creature millions of years old provides eggs on which birds are dependent and provides in its blood a component depended on by *Homo sapiens*. How cool is that?"

The larvae molt four times inside the egg, then hatch after two to four weeks and dig their way out of the sand. They will molt three or four times a year for a few years and then, at age five or six, molt annually. Males become sexually mature in their eighth or ninth year, females in their tenth. By then they are sixteen to twenty inches in length and ten to twelve inches across. Those that make it through all that—and only a thousandth of 1 percent of the eggs will survive through the first year, according to Wenner—are thought to live for as long as thirty years.

Horseshoe crabs are nocturnal, which helps them avoid predators such as shorebirds as well as sharks and loggerhead turtles. When the latter are present, horseshoe crabs often bury themselves in the sand, using the leaf-like ends of the last of seven pairs of legs. The five pairs between this and the pair at the front, used for feeling, are used for locomotion, as are the gills of juveniles. Those gills, in five pairs under the abdomen, absorb oxygen from the water and can be used for breathing on land if they remain moist.

Besides research and medical use, humans use horseshoe crabs as bait and in fertilizer. They were once used in animal feed. Recent regulations, fortunately, have reduced our harvest by as much as 80 percent.

"The near-term threat to horseshoe crabs is unsustainable harvest," says Wenner. "Harvest regulations instituted over the past fifteen years at national, coastwide, and state levels show signs of reversing past declines, which occurred over much of its range. Regulations are particularly effective in preventing local extinctions in the mid-Atlantic region, where major declines occurred. The long-term and emerging threat is habitat loss. Current habitat appears sufficient to support robust populations; however, habitat conditions could change as coastlines are developed and impacted by climate change."

A species of horseshoe crab once common to Japanese waters is endangered, and groups in the United States like the Atlantic States Marine Fisheries Commission are working to try to prevent that here, seeking to conserve a species whose very existence has been of untold value to our own and whose unique blend of features offers us such a compelling glimpse at life's myriad possibilities.

Atlantic Horseshoe Crab

DESCRIPTION: Up to a foot across; oval-shaped, helmet-like prosoma, or head; smaller abdomen; sword-like tail.

RANGE AND HABITAT: From Maine to the Yucatan and the northern Gulf of Mexico. Sandy, muddy beaches.

VIEWING TIPS: Horseshoe crabs are nocturnal. Spring spawning brings them ashore.

Crayfish

My first dose of the birds and bees came from a crayfish. Reddish-brown, looking like little lobsters, crayfish were an endless source of fascination in an idyllic childhood world of trails and tree houses, slingshots and pocket-knives. We slogged all day through creeks and ponds, clambered over fallen tree trunks, chased frogs and polliwogs, made spears and hatchets, imitated bird calls, collected leaves, and did a thousand other things that helped us learn about the world around us.

One of those was lifting rocks in the cold, clear water of the creek, watching crayfish scurry amid the sediment stirred up. Catching them was labor intensive, but we had nothing but time. Mostly we'd just inspect them, watching the four pairs of walking legs and those great pincers wave in agitation.

On this particular morning, we brought back a large one in a bucket and dumped it into an old tin washtub in the yard. The water was clear and when we put our hands in, the crayfish raised those claws like twin buckets on a backhoe, holding us at bay. I studied it for the longest time and eventually noticed a tiny one beside it. How had I missed it? Then there was another, and another, and another. Finally, it dawned on my seven-year-old brain that this was a mother producing babies right then and there. Reproduction 101 was under way.

Depending on where you are, they may be called crayfish, crawfish, crawdads, or mudbugs. Freshwater crustaceans that are related to the lobsters they favor, they are famously served up in the Cajun cuisine of Louisiana, where they're "the most valuable fishery in the state, with more than a hundred million pounds a year bringing in $185 million annually," according to Dr. Chris Bonvillain, associate professor and graduate program coordinator of the Department of Biological Sciences at Nicholls State University in Thibodaux, Louisiana. The city of Breaux Bridge, Louisiana, two hours to the west, is in fact known as the Crawfish Capital of the World and has hosted the Breaux Bridge Crawfish Festival every May since 1960.

Crayfish, though, have a much wider reach.

"There are almost seven hundred species and subspecies in the world," says Dr. Bonvillain. "Over 380 of those species, more than half of all crayfish species in the world, are located in North America, with more than 330 of those found in the southeastern United States, making us a crayfish biodiversity hotspot. Alabama has the highest diversity, with 97 species at last check."

Ranging in size from one and a half to nearly six inches long in the Southeast (and from less than an inch to thirty-one inches long worldwide), they can be found in most reasonably clean creeks, ponds, swamps, and lakes—and even in upland areas, where they burrow to find groundwater, leaving telltale mud chimneys. All are members of the family Cambaridae, and they have adapted to any number of niches. Some exist in just a few streams or a single cave system, while others are fairly widespread, with the red swamp crayfish, *P. clarkii*, according to Dr. Bonvillain, "probably one of the most abundant in the Southeast." Native to Louisiana, Arkansas, Mississippi, Alabama, Tennessee, Kentucky, and Florida, it has been introduced—originally by the Natural Resources Conservation Service—for aquaculture in Georgia, the Carolinas, and Virginia. It is, says Bonvillain, "one of the worst invasive species in the U.S. and Europe." Invasives are, of course, one of the natural world's major problems, and invasive crayfish have been known to spread diseases and outcompete and even extirpate native species.

The life histories and extent of distribution of many types of crayfish remain a mystery, and species are still being discovered. Even identification can be difficult. Some have distinctive markings or colorings—they can range from greenish-yellow to blue—but many are reddish brown and can be distinguished only by microscopic examination of mature male individuals in certain phases of the breeding cycle.

Crayfish have segmented bodies with joined head and thorax packaged in a hard exoskeleton. Their legs have fracture plains along which they can be broken and, at the time of the next molt, regenerated. Their muscular tails, as my friends and I well knew, are powerful enough to provide quick rearward escape. They have both short and long antennae that are highly sensitive to odors and compound eyes attached to stalks.

As with all crayfish, says Bonvillain, "their gills do not collapse in air and allow crayfish to breathe atmospheric oxygen as long as the gills remain moist."

Many live under rocks and debris on the bottoms of their aquatic homes, and they're omnivores, scavenging for living and dead plant and animal matter. They can tear up larger pieces of food with those outsized claws, or chelipeds, and propel the smaller pieces to their mouths with smaller specialized appendages.

Their reproductive organs are internal, with genital pores located in the male at the base of the last pair of legs and in the female at the third. Some specimens have the organs of both. The male has two pairs of modified swimmerets under the tail that transfer sperm to a structure on the female's belly. She will lay from fewer than one hundred to seven hundred eggs, depending on her size and species. Eggs are passed through the sperm, fertilized, and attached under her tail. They hatch after a couple of weeks, and the young stay under the tail through two molts, then gradually head out on their own, looking like tiny versions of the adults—that was the point at which I saw them. At this point they are preyed on by insects, small fishes, and other crayfish, and they will eventually serve as food for snakes, turtles, birds, mammals such as otters and raccoons, and fish, including many game fish.

Growth means regular molting, and as a crayfish prepares to molt, it absorbs calcium from its shell, depositing it in two white "stones" on its head. When it sheds its exoskeleton, it is vulnerable until its soft, flexible covering hardens, relying on the calcium from those stones. It may well eat its shell after shedding it.

Their wide and long-standing presence (their fossils go back 150 million years) has long been a source of interest, and study of similar species in widely divergent locales was one step leading to the theory of plate tectonics, which introduced the notion that massive plates on the earth's surface move and that the continents were once connected.

Crayfish are not as sensitive to environmental pollutants as freshwater mussels but are nevertheless bellwethers of our often-troubled relationship with nature, susceptible to the kinds of poisons that have long run into our waterways from fields and lawns. Habitat loss is a concern, as it is with so many creatures. The U.S. Fish and Wildlife Service lists five species as federally endangered and more than fifty-five species as under review.

There are practical things we can do to help protect crayfish, some as simple as not dumping them from bait buckets into waters other than those where we got them. These are creatures we normally don't give much thought, but there is much we can learn by studying them, and anything capable of providing wonder and education for a child is surely worth preserving.

Crayfish

DESCRIPTION: Like tiny lobsters, 1.5–6 inches in adult length in the Southeast. Range of colors, most reddish brown.
RANGE AND HABITAT: Bodies of standing or flowing water. Some burrow into the ground. Found throughout the Southeast.
VIEWING TIPS: Under rocks or debris in creeks. Burrowing crayfish will make their presence known in damp yards.

Starfish

We've talked before about the fact that a lot of things aren't named very well: a guinea pig isn't a pig, a killer whale isn't a whale, and a flying lemur isn't a lemur—it can't fly, either.

Seldom, however, will you find scientists trying to change those common names. They avoid confusion by using the more precise Linnaean system of Latinized names and leave terms like "mayfly" and "June bug" to the rest of us.

In the case of starfish, though, there is a genuine kerfuffle under way. Many biologists want us to call them sea stars, since they're not fish, although the word "starfish" has been used in English since 1538, when "fish" counted for pretty much anything in the water. They were already called sea stars in other Western languages, and that term reached English by 1569. The matter is complicated by the fact that they're not always star shaped.

A very knowledgeable, occasionally very funny invertebrate zoologist/marine biologist named Christopher Mah (www.echinoblog.blogspot.com) terms this, only partly in jest, "a topic that has found bitter and vicious debate at museums, aquariums, marine biology, and even paleontology programs around the world!" He then throws in an additional bit of seasoning: technically, the proper common term for this group is "asteroid," from the family's Linnaean name Asteroidea (*astra* being Latin for "stars"), which he prefers to use. Somehow, though, adding as a third option a name associated with space objects doesn't seem as helpful as it could be.

I'm doubting that "sea star" is going to replace "starfish" for the average beachgoer any time soon (remember the effort to get us to use the metric system?), but while it's being sorted out, we might try to appreciate one of the sea's more amazing denizens.

The starfish is an echinoderm, one of about seven thousand sea creatures that include sea urchins, sand dollars, and sea cucumbers. There are more than 1,900 species of starfish, with hundreds in both the Gulf and the Atlantic, many of those in deeper waters, but just a relative handful common in near-shore, shallow-water habitats. They include:

- Royal sea star (*Astropecten articulatus*), slender-armed and smooth-skinned; purple and outlined with pale orange plates and small white spines along the edge; they are eight inches across and are found on sandy bottoms at depths up to five hundred feet from Chesapeake Bay to Colombia;

- Forbes' common star (*Asterias forbesi*), with thicker, stubbier arms; reddish brown to purple with brilliant orange madreporites (openings to the vascular system); they are seven to ten inches across and are found at depths up to 150 feet from Maine to Texas;

- Striped/lined sea star (*Luidia clathrata*), slender-armed, bluish gray with a dark strip down the center and a cream-colored mouth; they are eight to twelve inches across and are found in offshore mud or sand at depths up to about 125 feet, from New Jersey to Brazil.

"*Luidia clathrata*," says Mah, "is present on sandy bottoms in abundance and seems to be one of the more easily encountered species. Sometimes during really stormy seasons they will also get washed up on shore."

Worldwide, starfish live at virtually all temperatures and depths, range from less than half an inch to just over three feet in diameter and sport up to forty-four arms or none at all, in the case of some pentagonal species. These are brightly colored, spiny-skinned animals with plenty of interesting attributes—they lack brains and blood, they can regrow lost limbs, and many can take their stomachs to a meal rather than vice versa.

They are most commonly found with five radial arms, each containing pretty much every system—vascular, tactile, locomotive, and reproductive. The vascular system, which uses hydraulics to pump seawater rather than blood through the starfish, helps circulate needed and waste gases and, because it can be used to swell each arm and facilitate contact with surfaces or prey, aids in locomotion and feeding.

Most starfish reproduce sexually. Each arm houses two gonads that release sperm or egg cells through openings between the arms, with fertilization external in most species. Many of the resulting larvae live as one component of the floating organic mass known as plankton, although some may be found under rocks. The larvae develop into brachiolaria, which settle onto and attach themselves to the seabed before undergoing metamorphosis, then detach themselves as tiny juveniles, just a millimeter in diameter.

There is another form of reproduction that stems from the fact that starfish can regenerate themselves from fragments by a process of cloning, regrowing arms or even, when split, forming two complete organisms.

The central disc contains the business ends of the digestive system. The mouth, at the center of the disc bottom, leads to a two-part stomach and a short intestine to an anus at the center of the top.

"Feeding in starfishes is diverse," says Mah. "Several species feed on mussels, clams, and oysters, but other species feed on sponges, corals, algae, and other colonial or encrusting organisms." They detect odor with chemoreceptors and have simple eyespots at the ends of their arms, both helpful in locating food. They can crawl in the direction of prey, and those that eat bivalves use sticky pads that look like but aren't suction cups on their arms to force open the shells. Many, like *Asterias,* can extrude their stomachs through their mouths and into the shell opening, surrounding the meal and secreting digestive juices from glands in their arms. The stomach is then retracted and the food passed to the pyloric stomach, which remains inside. Others, including *Astropecten* and *Luidia,* swallow their prey whole and start to digest it in their cardiac stomachs, excreting what is undigestible.

They have few natural enemies, as the spiny plates on their surface discourage many predators, but some gulls, fish, king crabs, sea otters, and even other starfish are known to eat them.

"Many sea stars have spines and heavy armor," says Mah, "but others have toxic chemicals in their body wall, which make them unpalatable. Some, such as the slime star, *Pteraster,* can emit a noxious slime or mucus as a defense."

They have, though, been subject to outbreaks of Starfish Wasting Disease, which has affected species on both U.S. coasts in recent years. The attendant die-offs followed population explosions and seem to be tied to climate change.

Higher temperatures are precisely what is predicted by many present-day climate models, and Mah says that will be "an increasing problem for all echinoderms, affecting everything from the behavior, larval growth, food, and thus ecology and structure of the community. In addition, increased acidity in the world's oceans will have significant effects on the skeletons of starfishes and other echinoderms."

It is incumbent upon us as wildlife watchers to be informed and engaged when it comes to our impact on the world and to set our appreciation for these remarkable creatures and their simple yet uncommon beauty within that larger framework.

Starfish (Sea Star, Asteroid)

DESCRIPTION: From one-quarter inch to 4 feet across, generally though not always star-shaped. From drab to brightly colored.
RANGE AND HABITAT: Virtually throughout the world's oceans. On both sandy and rocky stretches of shore, to great depths. Three species common: royal sea star; Forbes' common star; striped or lined sea star.
VIEWING TIPS: Beaches; most often seen when washed onshore after winter storms.

Atlantic and Gulf Sturgeon

Beauty, like success, is a matter of perspective, and sometimes the concepts intertwine. At the end of a boxing match, you don't have to be pretty; you just have to be standing. On an evolutionary scale, the single best measure of success and, arguably, of beauty is longevity.

That makes the sturgeon, cosmetics aside, one of the world's more beautiful creatures. It has, after all, been slurping clams, snails, worms, and crustaceans from ocean and river bottoms since 150 million years before a giant comet wiped out the dinosaurs. It is a true marvel of adaptation whose tale of survival soured only in the past century or two, thanks, as you might expect, to *Homo sapiens*.

Built like a shark-catfish hybrid, the Atlantic sturgeon, one of twenty-seven species worldwide, is noteworthy first of all for its size. A specimen that washed up on Folly Beach south of Charleston in March 2012 brought "sea monster" headlines. These days, a large one can reach eight feet in length and weigh three hundred pounds, and the largest ever recorded was fourteen feet long and weighed eight hundred pounds. Its relative, the Eurasian beluga sturgeon, has reached twenty-four feet and more than 3,500 pounds.

The Atlantic sturgeon is found in rivers and coastal waters from Labrador to northern Florida. In the 2012 Endangered Species Act listing for Atlantic sturgeon, National Oceanic and Atmospheric Administration (NOAA) Fisheries defined the South Atlantic distinct population segment (DPS) as containing those spawning in nine river systems from the Edisto in South Carolina to the St. Marys in Florida. The Carolina DPS contains those spawning in up to twelve river systems from the Roanoke in North Carolina to the Cooper in South Carolina. A subspecies, the Gulf sturgeon, virtually indistinguishable from the Atlantic, spawns in seven rivers from the Suwannee in Florida to the Pearl in Louisiana. Its range prior to its exploitation as a commercial fish probably extended to the Rio Grande.

The sturgeon has a bony, ancient look, as though it had been hewn roughly from stone. It is bluish-black or olive brown with paler sides and a white belly, with a dorsal fin sitting well back near its shark-like tail. Its skeleton, like that of sharks, is mostly cartilaginous.

"Sturgeon are really cool in this way," says Jason Kahn, with NOAA's Office of Protected Resources in Maryland. "They're classified as bony fish because they had a bony skeleton at one point and have, through convergent evolution, reached a cartilaginous state similar to sharks via a very different evolutionary path."

This is a bottom feeder that uses its snout and four sensitive, whisker-like barbels to probe sand and mud. It sucks food into a soft, toothless mouth it can extend like a camera lens, expels silt and gravel through its gills, and grinds the meal up in a gizzard-like stomach.

The sturgeon was here in abundance when European settlers arrived and had long been harvested by Native Americans. Some considered it a nuisance, since its five rows of bony plates, called scutes, could tear up nets, but eventually people warmed to it. Its meat became a cheap, popular alternative to smoked salmon, its skin yielded leather used in clothing and bookbinding, and its swim bladders provided isinglass, a gelatinous substance used in clarifying glue and jelly, beer and wine.

And then there was caviar. The salted eggs of the sturgeon were a delicacy in Europe, and American fishermen were happy to serve those markets. By the late 1800s, we exported seven million pounds of sturgeon yearly, with individual fish averaging three hundred pounds. But overfishing, on their spawning grounds and winter feeding grounds, quickly took a toll, as did dams, dredging, and pollution. Tampa Bay, a winter feeding ground, was stripped of sturgeon in just three years, from 1887 to 1889, by commercial fishermen. In 1905, the national catch had plummeted to twenty thousand pounds.

Small-scale commercial and recreational harvests limped along for half a century, but by 1940 in South Carolina, for instance, the average sturgeon caught weighed just seventy-five pounds, and the harvest was a mere ton and a half, down from a quarter of a million pounds. In 1972, Alabama became the first state to impose a ban on any harvest of sturgeon. Other states followed suit on both the Atlantic and the Gulf coasts, with some banning entanglement nets as well. The federal government placed the Gulf sturgeon on the endangered species list in 1991 and the Atlantic sturgeon in 2012; in 1998, the Atlantic States Marine Fisheries Commission (ASMFC) enacted a moratorium on the harvest or possession of Atlantic sturgeon.

The problem is not unique to the Americas. Worldwide, twenty-three of the twenty-seven sturgeon species are endangered, making it one of the world's most threatened groups of animals. Part of the challenge is that sturgeon reproduce slowly. Experts have disagreed on the age of sexual maturity, with anywhere from five to twelve cited for Southeast Atlantic sturgeon males, with eight years as the average, and seven to fifteen for females. As for frequency, males are thought to spawn every one to three years, with many accounts suggesting they spawn annually, and females spawn from every two to five years, with latitude a factor; sturgeon can live to about thirty years in the Southeast Atlantic and up to sixty years or so in the northern part of their range, with correspondingly later sexual maturity.

In general, along the northern Atlantic coast, sturgeon are spring spawners. In the southern Atlantic, they spawn in the fall, with reports of spring spawning in South Carolina's Edisto and Virginia's James rivers. As for Gulf sturgeon, NOAA's Joe Heublein asserts they are spring spawners, "although there may be some preliminary evidence of fall spawning in some parts of their range."

Despite the volumes that remain to be uncovered about the process, it's clear the figures associated with sturgeon reproduction are impressive. "Fecundity has been correlated with age and body size," says Bill Post, diadromous fishes coordinator with the South Carolina Department of Natural Resources, "so it can be highly variable, but generally 500,000 to 1.5 million eggs is a safe estimate. Not long ago, a tugboat strike in Delaware killed a gravid female, and the folks there pulled out fifty-three pounds of roe, an entire five-gallon bucket full."

Females will choose a spot well upriver. "Spawning location is closely associated with larval drift distance," says Kahn. "They simply can't spawn in a location that would subject larvae to salinity—at least not if they want their offspring to survive."

The male releases sperm as the female lays eggs, and many, though not all, are fertilized. The fertilized eggs are sticky and adhere to gravel or rock on the stream bottom. Embryos consume their yolk sacs for a week or two until reaching the larval stage, and eggs and larvae wash downstream, with larvae often settling in backwaters; they feed on insect larvae and tiny crustaceans, reaching seven or eight inches in length and moving back into the river proper.

They spend between one and five years in their natal systems before leaving to migrate along the coast. They are often three to four feet in length when they first move into the ocean, and tagging data indicate they travel widely once they emigrate.

As for the spawning females, a NOAA overview says those in the Southeast Atlantic population "typically exit the rivers within four to six weeks after spawning," with males remaining longer. They winter in the Gulf or the Atlantic from October or November through March or April. Gulf sturgeon oversummer around freshwater springs and migrate back to estuaries in the fall.

Young sturgeon are fed on by eagles, ospreys, barred owls, catfish, and alligators, among others, with only sharks and alligators prepared to take on the adults. They are susceptible to some parasites, but the impact of these on the overall health of the sturgeon population is thought to be minimal.

There are plenty of other concerns. Sturgeon are a bycatch in some commercial fishing methods, particularly gillnets, are susceptible to ship and boat strikes, and are affected by water quality (pollution and red tide, for example), dredging, and dams.

A five-year review released in 2009 by the U.S. Fish and Wildlife Service and the National Marine Fisheries Service noted that Gulf populations in most river systems were thought to be in the hundreds, with just the Suwannee and Choctawhatchee populations in the thousands. Overall, it cited stable or slightly increasing populations in Florida, with a strong uptick in the Suwannee, where a 1984 harvest ban has helped spur a dramatic rebound, with the population thought to be approaching twenty thousand individuals. That has presented its own problems, as sturgeon are known to jump from the water—one struck and killed a five-year-old girl on the Suwannee in 2015.

"South Carolina never fully agreed that Atlantic sturgeon were declining, at least in some rivers," adds NOAA's Andy Herndon. "It is clear they are in decline in certain rivers along the Atlantic Coast, but the Winyah Bay System, Edisto River, and Savannah River seem to have stable populations and minimal impact from anthropogenic factors."

A 2017 report by the ASMFC cited "a stable to slowly increasing population of Atlantic sturgeon," though Kahn urges caution, citing sparse data. We can hope, given the sturgeon's track record, that a bit of optimism is not out of order.

"Sturgeon have enjoyed a long run for a variety of reasons," says Heublein, "including broad environmental tolerances, long lifespan, and high fecundity. What this means is sturgeon can hunker down when times are bad and still produce a large number of progeny when times are good."

As for the pressure from our taste for caviar, most caviar worldwide is now a product of aquaculture, including operations in North Carolina, Georgia, and Florida. We can only hope that changes in tastes and our relationship to wild places can spell a brighter future for this otherwise beautifully adapted living fossil.

Atlantic and Gulf Sturgeon

DESCRIPTION: Bluish-black to green, lighter sides, white belly, snout with barbels; 5 rows of bony scutes rather than scales.

RANGE AND HABITAT: River bottoms when very young, spawning, or oversummering (for the Gulf species). Estuaries when juveniles.

Otherwise, ocean dwellers; Gulf sturgeon are found in the Gulf of Mexico. VIEWING TIPS: Rarely sighted. This is one best read about or viewed as part of your favorite nature series.

Endangered Species Permit #16442

Manatee

On January 9, 1493, near the end of his first voyage to the new world, Christopher Columbus noted that he and his crew had seen three mermaids. They were, he said, "not half as beautiful as they are painted."

Given that they were likely manatees or their relatives, that's not surprising. There is a lot to love about manatees—they are gentle, slow moving, graceful, and curious—but you would be hard pressed to mistake one of these chubby, seal-like mammals with a mug like a walrus's for a mermaid. And yet, in one of nature's charmingly head-scratching twists, they are members of the order Sirenia, a name taken from the sirens said to lure seamen to their deaths.

The order currently has four members—three species of manatee, the Amazonian, the African, and ours, the West Indian; and the dugong, a relative found in the Indian Ocean. The Florida manatee, one of two subspecies of the West Indian, may be found in the summer sporadically north "into the Carolinas and even on occasion as far as Massachusetts," says Bob Bonde, longtime research scientist for the Sirenia Project of the U.S. Geological Survey in Gainesville, Florida, "and west into the Gulf of Mexico, in Alabama, Mississippi, and Texas."

Most summer dispersal occurs from late April through mid-October, when the water temperature is at or above 68 degrees. In winter months, manatees return to Florida, where they can be found in bays, estuaries, rivers and canals, since they are tolerant of salt, fresh, or brackish water.

Manatees are plant-eaters, and what looks like chubbiness is simply the ample space required for up to 150 feet of hindgut fermenting intestines that use bacteria to break down what your grandmother called roughage. That process produces, as it does in cattle, plenty of gas. For biologists studying manatees, which may dine or rest underneath ten feet of murky water, that has a distinct advantage. Just ask Al Segars, stewardship coordinator at ACE Basin National Estuarine Research Reserve.

"When we were monitoring manatees on the Cooper River, we were looking for gas bubbles to locate them. It's a good sign—it suggests they've been eating and their GI tract is functioning." The alternative involves waiting for them to bob up to the surface to take a breath, normally at three- to five-minute intervals, although they can stay under for twenty minutes if needed.

Actually, since decomposing plants on the bottom also release gas, manatees, in dislodging them, can release bubbles that way. And they are steady diners, eating up to 10 percent of their body weight in sea grass a day. Their split upper lips, with each side essentially prehensile, can grasp and manipulate vegetation like a hand as they dig up rooted plants with their flippers. Large salivary glands begin digestion, kicking off a week-long journey through those long intestines. Their erupted teeth—six to seven on each side of the upper and lower jaw—have flat grinding surfaces, and as those in front are worn down, "the row of advancing molars moves steadily forward like a conveyor belt at about one millimeter per month," according to Bonde, "with new ones being produced constantly from the rear—as an endless supply of teeth is very beneficial for a manatee that feeds on abrasive material."

Females in Florida may go into heat during the warmer months when the available vegetation starts growing, and males pick up the chemical signal, often following in herds that may compete for weeks as they try to breed with the focal female. A female often flees until she's receptive, then couples briefly with one or more males, abdomen to abdomen. Males have no role in the calves' upbringing.

Gestation lasts a little more than a year, and the female gives birth underwater to one (rarely, two) four-foot-long calf weighing sixty to seventy pounds. She helps it to the surface for its first breath, and within an hour it's swimming on its own. The young are born with teeth and begin nibbling on grasses in three weeks or so.

"The mother will bond with her calf," says Bonde, "a process that ensures it will remain with her for the next couple of years, a period in which the calf is dependent on her. Without that care, its chance of survival is much lower. In many cases, rescued calves have been orphaned, or separated due to the inexperience of first-time calving moms, or lack of due diligence in maintaining the bond, due to boat traffic or noise. With that care, the calf will learn how to meet the challenges of surviving on its own. The experience calves gain from mothers helps prepare them for remembering where important necessary habitat is—finding warmth, fresh water, feeding sites, migration routes, et cetera."

The female is larger than the male, and the largest manatee on record weighed 3,600 pounds and was fifteen feet long, although 1,200 pounds and ten feet are more common for an adult. They have very thick skin for protection from the environment, with a thin layer of fat beneath. They are surprisingly agile, capable of somersaults, head and tail stands, barrel rolls, and upside-down gliding. Their hearing is quite good, but they have poor eyesight, although catlike whiskers thinly distributed all over their bodies help alert them to objects in the water. Their paddle-shaped flippers have three or four nails at the tips to protect them, but they have no hind limbs, as these have been lost during their evolution from land to water sixty million years ago. They still have vestigial pelvic bones.

"Their brains are about the size of a grapefruit," says Bonde, "with few of the folds associated with higher intelligence. However, manatees are very smart animals and use their brains to remember experiences during their long lives. They bring to mind the adage we use for their relatives, the elephants—manatees appear never to forget!"

They communicate with sight, taste, touch, and sound, with squeals, chirps, and whistles all part of their vocalizations when frightened, annoyed, playing, or aroused. They rarely fight and display little fear, an insouciance born of evolution amid ample food resources and no natural enemies. Humans are the main problem. The manatee's buoyancy—the result of heavy bones that provide ballast, lungs that run the length of their backs, and the gas they make digesting their food—and their love of shallow water bring them into contact with people. And, says Bonde, "we continue to encroach into their aquatic world."

"There's a big problem with people watering and feeding them," adds Segars (both practices are prohibited by federal law). "Everyone wants to 'befriend' them and get a video for Facebook or YouTube. It's not malice on the part of the public, but they have to be aware that they are reinforcing the behavior of hanging around docks and marinas. That greatly increases the risk of boat strikes."

They can also get caught in or eat monofilament line, which clogs their digestive systems. Herbicide runoff and pollution, development, and dredging can eliminate food and habitat. They have also been known to swim upriver and get through locks at dam sites, making them unable to continue their migration and susceptible to hypothermia with the onset of winter.

Natural causes like cold weather and red tide, a harmful algal bloom, can kill them, and their attraction to warm water runoff from power plants and the like further heightens their vulnerability.

Manatees were first protected in Florida in 1893 and became one of the original seventy-eight species listed as threatened with extinction by the Endangered Species Preservation Act of 1966. The U.S. Fish and Wildlife Service, charged with conserving, protecting, and enhancing fish, wildlife, plants, and their habitats, listed the manatee as endangered a year later. Conservation efforts have helped, and manatees are currently doing well. Their numbers are increasing in Florida— there are six thousand or so, up from fewer than three thousand in 2007 and just a few hundred in 1967. Rangewide, in the area including Puerto Rico, Mexico, Central America and the Antilles, there are an estimated seven thousand more, although little is known specifically about the populations of manatees outside the United States.

In 2017, thanks to those improvements, the U.S. Fish and Wildlife Service downlisted the species' status from endangered to threatened, while stating that existing protective measures would remain in place.

Overall, Segars counsels us to be wildlife watchers, not minglers.

"Wild animals do not need to be our 'friends,'" he says. "They need a healthy fear of humans. Manatees do not need fresh water from a hose; they did quite well for thousands of years without water from humans. Such behavior is not only illegal but also has a very negative impact on these animals. Enjoy them from a distance!"

West Indian Manatee, *Trichechus manatus;* Florida Manatee, *Trichechus manatus latirostris*

DESCRIPTION: 10–12 feet long, 800–1,200 pounds; gray/brown, gentle and slow moving.

RANGE AND HABITAT: West Indian ranges from northern South America to mid-Atlantic coast when water, whether salt, fresh, or brackish, is warm.

VIEWING TIPS: Near shore and in inlets in warm months.

Eastern Oyster

It's not hard to overlook some of the species that most impact our lives. Honeybees, pollinators imported from Europe, are at the heart of much of our food production. Bats are invaluable pest-control devices. Then there is the eastern oyster, which shapes its environment as few species do.

"Oysters are ecosystem engineers," says Nancy Hadley, retired biologist with the South Carolina Department of Natural Resources. "They build habitat, they control water quality, they modify their environment. They are keystone species, like coral reefs," which were once the dominant component of estuaries worldwide.

Eastern oysters, found from Canada to Central America along the Atlantic and Gulf shores, were once staggeringly abundant. In the 1880s, we pulled twenty million bushels a year out of Chesapeake Bay alone. Now, thanks to the overharvesting, pollution, habitat loss, and dredging that affect oysters worldwide, the Bay yields one-hundredth that amount.

"If oysters are removed," says Hadley, "the entire ecosystem will change. This has happened in the Chesapeake Bay." An adult oyster can filter fifty gallons of water in a day. When they were plentiful, the Bay's oysters could filter an amount equal to the Bay's entire volume in a few days. Now, it would take a year.

As filter feeders, oysters draw in seawater over their gills with beating, hair-like cilia. Nondigestible particles are bound up in mucus and expelled as "pseudofeces," nutrient-rich strings that are an important part of the food chain for bottom-dwellers like polychaete worms. Desirable particles, predominantly single-celled algae called phytoplankton, are transported to the mouth, then through the esophagus and stomach to the anus. The liver and heart do about what ours do, the latter pumping clear, colorless blood through the body to two waste-removing kidneys. Two pairs of nerve cords and three pairs of ganglia make up the nervous system. All of that is lumped inside the mantle, two fleshy folds secreting the shells and playing a role in respiration and excretion.

Eating all that may not sound appetizing, but humans have been ingesting oysters, to judge from archeological finds, for well over 100,000 years, with Americans currently consuming 2.5 billion of them a year. The U.S. fishery is dominated by Louisiana, which produces about 50 percent of the total U.S. harvest, with Texas and Virginia together contributing another 25 percent.

A 2011 Nature Conservancy study that paints a grim picture worldwide rates reef conditions in much of the Gulf as fair and those along most of the Atlantic coast as poor or functionally extinct.

A century ago, canneries and shucking houses dumped shells back into the beds each year, providing new generations with "replanted" habitat. Now, with oysters sold primarily to restaurants or individuals, Hadley says, "the need for restocking is as great or greater than ever, but the shells are harder to come by." As a result, many states have sponsored shell recycling programs to try to recapture postconsumer shells for replanting. Such programs rely heavily on public participation to return shells, with state agencies or nonprofits often collecting from restaurants and caterers as well.

The eastern oyster is one of five oyster species consumed in the United States and one of many worldwide that fall into the edible, pearl, and windowpane categories, the latter often used for decorative purposes. The Eastern has a variably shaped shell with three layers formed largely of calcium carbonate extracted from seawater and combined with protein. The inner layer is the pearly nacre, though pearl oysters are from another family. The rough, stony outer layer ranges from dirty white to dark gray. The carbon that oysters extract for their shells helps reduce the amount that can return to the atmosphere as the greenhouse gas carbon dioxide, and calcium carbonate helps fight ocean acidification, which is currently devastating coral reefs.

Oyster reefs are formed as larvae cement themselves to the shells of adult oysters, building a bed providing habitat for many small organisms and the creatures that feed on them and making oyster reefs excellent fishing spots. In those areas where they occur intertidally, oyster reefs form natural breakwaters that help protect against erosion.

Eastern oysters are sexually dimorphic—there are separate sexes—but each winter the reproductive organs wither, to regenerate in the spring, at which point oysters can change from one sex to the other. During their first year, most oysters spawn as male. With growth, most change into females. In late spring and throughout the summer, rising water temperatures trigger males to release sperm, stimulating females to release eggs by the millions.

"It is a privileged observer indeed who happens to witness this phenomenon," says Hadley. "I have only seen it once. It took me a few minutes to realize what was happening. The entire water column over the oyster bed turned milky white with millions, perhaps billions, of eggs and sperm."

Fertilized eggs develop into fully planktonic larvae, feeding on phytoplankton, in twelve to twenty-four hours. These larvae drift with the currents for several weeks, most becoming food for fish. After two or three weeks they have doubled in size, have developed a foot and "eye spot," and are ready to find a hard surface to which they will cement.

"The young oyster can never relocate," says Hadley, "so selecting a good site is critical. For this reason, oyster larvae actively seek out adult oyster shells for attachment, providing reasonable assurance they are in a suitable location and will be near other oysters, a necessity for these broadcast spawners."

Oysters can reach a harvestable size of three inches in two years. They can live twenty years and reach eight inches in length, although, given harvesting pressure, they seldom live past five years. They might seem impervious to predators but are eaten by starfish, crabs, a snail called an oyster drill, boring sponges, and seabirds, including oystercatchers.

A growing trend in the oyster industry is mariculture, or oyster farming, which can produce high-quality oysters in twelve to eighteen months. Larvae are started in hatcheries, introduced to ground-up shells for attachment, and grown to market size in cages in suitable tidal creeks and estuaries. They can be bred for fast growth, desirable shell shape, disease resistance, even sterility, allowing them to devote all their energy to growth rather than reproduction.

Mariculture permits summer harvest, something that wasn't done traditionally, with oysters harvested and eaten only in months containing an *r*. With summer harvest, though, comes the increased risk of consumption-related illnesses, as oysters concentrate bacteria and viruses up to one hundred times the levels found in surrounding water. The warmer summer waters can also foster blooms of toxic dinoflagellates (red tides), which can cause oysters to become toxic.

With vigilance ideally as the watchword, we continue to eat eastern oysters by the billions, with oyster farming promising to increase production even if natural populations decline. A growing movement compares oysters to wines, with taste differences due to regional variations.

As for the notion of oysters as "watchable wildlife," Hadley points us in the right direction by speaking, oddly enough, about the process of expelling the seawater they've drawn in to extract nutrients.

"Oysters spit when the tide goes out," she says, "and again when it comes in. As far as I know, nobody knows why, but if you sit by an estuary or tidal creek on a quiet night, you can hear them. It's like a symphony."

If that doesn't qualify them, I don't know what would.

Eastern Oyster

DESCRIPTION: Calcium carbonate shells, dirty white to gray outside, pearly white nacre sometimes tinged with blue inside.

RANGE AND HABITAT: Atlantic and Gulf of Mexico. Subtidal estuarine areas through most of the range, but mostly intertidal along South Carolina and Georgia coasts.

VIEWING TIPS: Many oyster beds along the coast. Handle with care: those who work with them call them "nature's razors."

Striped Bass

Eggs are marvelous entities. Each contains a DNA-encoded recipe for turning food and water into a member of that species' next generation. Each is also a housing unit designed to encapsulate and nourish that individual for a brief time at the dawn of its life.

As crucial as that role is, eggs are, in general, quite fragile commodities. Even those with hard, protective shells are susceptible to mishap and breakage, and those without—well, they're commonly fated to become quick nourishment for some other species.

Animals that lay few eggs are likely to take extraordinary precautions. Birds may construct hard-to-reach nests and maintain bodily contact until well after the young hatch. Those that lay a lot of eggs can afford to be more cavalier about the process.

Many fish are, of course, in the latter group, and in the case of the striped bass, we can be talking extreme numbers. A female striper's fecundity increases with age and size, with a five-pounder releasing on the order of 25,000 eggs, a twelve-pounder a million, and a seventy-five-pounder three million, classically after an upriver migration. Anadromous striped bass migrate from salt to fresh water for spawning. Given the fact that a lot of other creatures are waiting to eat those eggs and the resulting fry and fingerlings, the odds of survival are miniscule. Still, in a stable population, if just two of those eggs on average develop and reach adulthood, that population can maintain equilibrium.

Four centuries ago, with little human pressure on the North Atlantic population of striped bass, that reproductive strategy made for incredible success. One member of the Massachusetts Bay Colony reported in 1614 that he had seen so many striped bass it seemed possible to walk across their backs without getting his shoes wet. Those who recall the saga of the passenger pigeon, though, know that humans are perfectly capable of laying waste to marvels of superabundance, and that nearly happened to the anadromous striped bass population along the Atlantic coast.

Overfishing was a recognized problem in some waterways in the seventeenth century, and it wiped out many of the great New England spawning runs by the late eighteenth. Today, fully 90 percent of the striped bass in New England waters are dependent upon Chesapeake Bay spawning grounds, with most of the rest utilizing the Hudson River.

There are two other kinds of striped bass populations—riverine, classically breeding in the major river systems south of Cape Hatteras to the St. John's River in Florida, and across the Gulf of Mexico; and inland, occurring mainly in reservoirs (or downstream of those reservoirs) and almost always supported by stocking.

Riverine and inland populations have also faced the challenges of fishing pressure, pollution, and development. Riverine populations were affected by dams built for flood control, power generation, and recreational use, some during the New Deal of the 1930s. The Santee-Cooper project in South Carolina, to take one example, produced 42 miles of dams and dikes as part of the largest earthmoving project in the nation's history to that point, creating Lake Marion and Lake Moultrie.

"Striped bass were trapped in Santee-Cooper's inland reservoirs," says Jim Bulak, retired fisheries biologist with the South Carolina Dept. of Natural Resources, "but because large rivers flowed into those reservoirs, the striped bass were able to successfully spawn and create a world-class fishery. Once this happened, scientists figured out how to artificially propagate this species and striped bass were stocked all over the U.S. and certain parts of the world." This accelerated a process that had begun as early as 1879, when East Coast stripers were stocked in San Francisco Bay.

For those that reproduce naturally, spawning is triggered by water temperature, occurring when it rises to 68° Fahrenheit for at least two or three days. Released eggs, carried away on currents, hatch after forty-eight hours or so, depending on water temperature. Those hatchlings develop mouthparts in about five days. They form small schools and move toward the shore, feeding at first on zooplankton, then on small crustaceans and mayflies. At one year, they are about a foot long. Adults, which primarily eat fish and invertebrates, move in schools and feed most actively in the morning and evening, reducing their feeding when the water temperature falls below 50° Fahrenheit.

Stripers are true bass, unlike largemouth and smallmouth, which are actually members of the sunfish family. They are greenish blue on the back, silvery on the sides and white beneath, with six to eight horizontal stripes. Males reach sexual maturity at two years, females at four years, depending on latitude, with those in more northern waters maturing later.

Their size and fighting ability make them extremely popular game fish, which is why they have been stocked in so many corners of the world. Both the federal government, which deals with the anadromous population, and state wildlife/conservation agencies, dealing with inland and riverine populations, have worked for decades to try to try to bring back and stabilize depleted striped bass numbers, and to foster the sustaining of stable populations, with size limits and catch quotas part of the picture, along with introduction, stocking, and hybridization.

In fact, the advent of the hybrid has changed the dynamic greatly. The hybrid striped bass was developed in 1965 by South Carolina fisheries biologist Bob Stevens, who crossed female striped bass with male white bass for a variant known as the original or palmetto hybrid striped bass. Hybrids (there are several varieties now) have been shown to have superior early growth rates, greater disease resistance, and improved survival rates, and they have been widely stocked in waters with unsuitable habitat for striped bass but suitable for a hybrid.

Suitability boils down primarily to one factor.

"Water quality is the most direct," says Bulak, "as striped bass cannot survive when either the water becomes too warm or it does not hold sufficient oxygen. Across the Southeast, a number of reservoirs have experienced striped bass die-offs intermittently or regularly. The combination of marginal habitat plus scarce food resources (e.g., Lake Norman, North Carolina) can also lead to a cessation of striped bass stocking in favor of hybrid striped bass, which can withstand warmer water a little better."

Poor conditions affect even a strategy designed to help sustain populations —catch-and-release.

"In the hottest parts of summer, especially in Southeastern reservoirs," says Bulak, "many caught and released striped bass will die, even though they initially appear to swim off. In general, the chance of catch and release mortality increases as water temperatures rise and the availability of oxygen-rich water decreases during the summer months."

Even cooler water in the deeper pockets of such a reservoir isn't a panacea, as the change in pressure when fish are pulled from this depth is itself problematic.

Still, there are healthy populations across much of its range, and the striped bass remains a favorite of sport fishermen and women. Age is the chief determiner of size, and the largest striper known was a 92-pounder netted by Maryland's Department of Natural Resources in 1995. The largest taken with rod and reel weighed 81 pounds 14 ounces and was 54 inches long. It was taken off the coast of Connecticut by an angler named Greg Myerson. The largest taken in fresh water was 45-½-inches long and weighed 69 pounds 9 ounces. It was taken in the Upper Blackhead Reservoir in Alabama by James Bramlett in 2013.

Striped Bass

DESCRIPTION: Greenish-blue back, silvery sides, white underbelly, with 6 to 8 horizontal stripes. Normally 2 to 20 pounds, with the female larger and heavier, they can reach much higher weights.
HABITAT AND RANGE: Stocked in many places in U.S. and around the world. Found along Eastern seaboard and northern Gulf of Mexico, and inland through the Mississippi Valley, and along the Pacific Coast.
VIEWING TIPS: Found in salt or fresh water, in major river systems and lakes.

Great White Shark

White sharks should not be high on your worry list. Yes, they can kill you, but in the United States, bees, dogs, cows, horses, and rattlesnakes—in that order—are much more likely to do you in. Recent noteworthy attacks and the apparent greater presence of sharks on some beaches notwithstanding, on average sharks cause fewer than one death per year in the United States. Worldwide, there are eighty-four unprovoked shark attacks per year on average over the last decade, with just a handful by great whites, resulting in an average of six fatalities. Lightning, by contrast, kills thousands of people worldwide each year.

And yet the great white is the Elvis of predators, thanks in great measure to the 1975 thriller *Jaws,* which changed the way we view them to this day.

Chris Fischer and like-minded colleagues are trying to change our minds back again.

"We've lost our connection to and awareness of the ocean," says Fischer, founding chairman and expedition leader of OCEARCH (combining "ocean" and "research") whose information-gathering voyages are aimed at "pioneering fundamental research on sharks." Observing that 200,000 sharks are taken per day (many for shark fin soup), Fischer views the situation as critical.

"If we lose our sharks," he says, "we lose the lions of the sea. They are key to healthy fish populations, since they cull the sick and weak, and when sharks are removed from the ecosystem, second-tier predator populations explode and wipe out the food chain below them. Unless great whites are thriving in the North Atlantic, there won't be fish to catch."

OCEARCH captures great whites, spends fifteen minutes tagging them with tracking devices and allowing scientists to draw blood and conduct additional research, then releases them. Tagging allows scientists and non-scientists alike to track whites in real time via maps on its website, www.ocearch.org, and mobile apps.

The work does have its detractors, who say the procedure is not without risk to the sharks. Still, scientists and journalists clamor to join its voyages and use its data, which show, among other things, the huge migratory loop North Atlantic whites—apparently mature pregnant females—undertake every two or three years.

"Thanks to tagged sharks and OCEARCH data," says Bryan Frazier, coastal shark biologist with the South Carolina Department of Natural Resources, "we're re-learning day by day. Among other things, it's showing there are multiple foraging areas in the summer off of Massachusetts and off of Nova Scotia, with a shared winter foraging area off the southeastern U.S."

"Apex predator" seems faint praise for this monarch of the sea. It can be twenty feet long and weigh five thousand pounds, although thirteen to sixteen feet and two thousand pounds are more common. It can cruise at ten to fifteen miles per hour and accelerate to thirty-five miles per hour.

Then there are those teeth—up to three hundred of them, triangular, razor-sharp, in rows that rotate forward as those in front break or wear off. In many species, the bottom teeth are better at gripping, the top at tearing. "In the white," says Frazier, "both upper and lower are designed for tearing." A white clamps down on prey, shaking its head side to side until it tears flesh loose, then swallows. "There's no chewing with sharks," adds Frazier.

This is an ambush hunter, taking prey from below. Its gray back helps it blend with rocky bottoms when viewed from above, while its white belly blends in with the brighter surface from below.

Directing it all is a brain weighing just ounces and primarily dedicated to smell, with a central cerebrum the size of a walnut. The rest is like a string of beads dedicated to separate functions.

This is a torpedo-shaped animal with a pointed snout, coal-black eyes, fins for balance, and a stiff, side-to-side swimming motion powered by a tail muscular enough to power leaps out of the water. The great white is one of more than a thousand species of sharks and rays that, unlike true fishes, have skeletons made of cartilage rather than bone. Their large oily livers help produce buoyancy in place of the gas-filled bladders many bony fish rely on, and they must keep moving to keep from sinking. Five gill slits on each side extract oxygen from the water, and the shark's muscles warm its blood, keeping the stomach, brain, and other organs eight to ten degrees warmer than the surrounding seawater. Its skin is made of dermal denticles, which are structurally homologous with teeth, although toughness is only one plus.

"Its advantage has more to do with fluid motion," says Frazier, "and how water passes across the skin. The era when all the competitive swimming records were being broken coincided with when swimsuit design was based on sharkskin."

The white's migratory route seems to have a built-in reproductive rhythm. Males have sperm-delivery organs called claspers extending from the pelvic fin. Bite marks on the backs, sides, and pectoral fins of females are thought to show that the somewhat smaller male grasps females with his teeth during coitus. Eggs hatch in utero, and embryos eat subsequently produced unfertilized eggs, as well as their own shed teeth, reutilizing calcium and other minerals. The female gives birth to from two to fourteen live pups, each three to five feet long, after gestation thought to take eleven months.

"Scientists have confirmed that a primary nursery area for white sharks is off the coast of New York and New Jersey," says Frazier. Females look for places with good food supply and relative safety but otherwise do not care for the young.

The young eat fish, rays, and other sharks until, when males are about ten feet long and females twelve to fourteen feet long, their jaws and teeth are strong enough to withstand the impact of biting adult-level prey. They are generalists and eat sea lions, seals, walruses, turtles, dolphins, tuna, other sharks, and whales, among other species. We're simply not on the menu—arms and legs are pretty bony—and most human bites are thought to be sharks using the only tool they have to figure out if we're edible. They can detect minute traces of blood from three miles away and have organs that sense the electromagnetic fields generated by prey's muscle contractions and heartbeat, down to one two-billionth of a volt.

With ancestors going back 400 million years, sharks have survived all five of the planet's mass extinctions. "Orcas have been observed killing white sharks," says Frazier, "but we don't know how common that is." As usual, we're the ones they have to worry about. They have been protected off South Africa, Australia, Canada, and the United States, are listed as "vulnerable" by the International Union for the Conservation of Nature, and are protected under some international agreements.

Fischer and OCEARCH will continue, as he says, "pouring the world's oceans into people's lives. I think we're exiting our infancy in terms of our knowledge of sharks. We are looking to break down barriers between academics and fishermen, and turn education and popular support toward affecting policy."

The stakes are immense.

"I can't overstate how important sharks are to the ocean's health," says Frazier. "A lot of fishermen hate sharks because they react to the signal put out by fish struggling on their hooks and go after them. Their brains are wired that way. That struggle tells the shark something is wrong, and that's the fish it culls. It's vital for the health of the target species. It's top-down control of the whole food web. If we didn't have sharks, we wouldn't have a healthy ocean."

Great White Shark

DESCRIPTION: Up to twenty feet long and five thousand pounds; sleek, gray above, white below.

RANGE AND HABITAT: Worldwide, between 60° north and 60° south. Wide migratory routes. Seasonally off southeastern coasts.

VIEWING TIPS: Watch for telltale fin at surface. Safest option: in front of your television set.

Acknowledgments

A book such as this involves a community. I want to thank first every one of the biologists, ecologists, educators, writers, photographers, and outdoorspeople whose experience, knowledge, and wisdom I sought and received in great measure. Thank you to those on the front lines of our state and national wildlife and conservation agencies. You are heroes.

In addition to those experts quoted in each section, Mary Bunch, Judy Barnes, and Jason Bettinger of the South Carolina Department of Natural Resources helped me with individual pieces. Thanks to the Florida Panther National Wildlife Refuge; Lilibeth Serran Vélez and Joe Madison, with the U.S. Fish and Wildlife Service; Tyler Bowling, manager of the Florida Program for Shark Research at the Florida Museum of Natural History; Nick Farmer, Frank Helies, and Allison Garrett of NOAA; Maggie Benally of the Navajo Office of Diné Culture and Language; Jeffrey Hostetler with the Florida Fish and Wildlife Conservation Commission; Fernanda Ubatuba, president and COO of OCEARCH; Dr. Bob Hueter, director of the Center for Shark Research at Mote Marine Laboratory; Ken Childs; Jim Kalisch; the University of Nebraska at Lincoln Dept. of Entomology; and Dr. Ric Bessin with the University of Kentucky. In every case, our conversations, by phone or e-mail, were invaluable and are appreciated.

Thank you to my editors at *South Carolina Wildlife*. Linda Renshaw asked me in 1994 whether I would be interested in doing a column for the magazine. "For Wildlife Watchers" has been a key part of my identity as a writer and one of the true joys of my writing life ever since. Many thanks to David Lucas and Caroline Foster and, most recently, to Joey Frazier, whose kindness and helpfulness have brought joy to my recent years with the column. I am grateful for his encouragement and support when it came to this book. Thank you too to Maria LaRocca, Kathryn Diaz, Tricia Way, Cindy Thompson, and to photographer Phillip Jones.

A special thank you to Richard Brown, who helms the University of South Carolina Press. I so appreciate your interest in this book and your openness to the give-and-take inherent in the author/press relationship in the course of negotiations, editing, and production. Thank you to the Press's Bill Adams, Pat Callahan, Suzanne Axland, Vicki Leach, MacKenzie Collier, Kerri Tolan, and Aurora Bell, and to copy editor Jeri Famighetti.

Thank you to my friends and colleagues in the Southeastern Outdoor Press Association and the Tennessee Outdoor Writers Association. You have taught me so much about the outdoors, about my profession, and about life. Many of my happiest moments have been in your presence.

And thank you to Debby, who opened up the world of the outdoors to me in a way it had never been open. Our bird walks, fishing trips, and picnics were where this all started, and you and our little white house in the country have been at the core of my identity since those days.

Contributing Wildlife Experts

I want to thank the following wildlife experts, whose work and research helped me immensely:

ANDREW ARNOLD is director of education and outreach at the Alabama Wildlife Center, a nonprofit focused on the care and conservation of wild birds in Pelham, Alabama. He holds a BS in wildlife sciences and a master's in biology. He is a native of southern Alabama.

DR. ERIC P. BENSON, Clemson University professor emeritus and extension entomologist, has responsibilities for research and education programs concerning household and structural pests in South Carolina. Dr. Benson's research interests are in integrated pest management (IPM) strategies for urban pests including ants, cockroaches, bedbugs, flies, and termites.

DR. RIC BESSIN has been extension entomologist at the University of Kentucky since 1991, working in the role of management of arthropod pests of field and specialty crops. He serves as the Integrated Pest Management Coordinator, Pesticide Safety Education Coordinator, and IR-4 minor Use Liaison for Kentucky.

DR. ROBERT BONDE is a retired federal research biologist with the U.S. Geological Survey and holds an adjunct faculty position at the graduate school of the University of Florida, College of Veterinary Medicine. Bob has studied manatees for forty years and specializes in their natural history, biology, genetics, and conservation. He has more than one hundred academic publications and has written a book with Dr. Roger Reep, *The Florida Manatee: Biology and Conservation.*

DR. CHRIS BONVILLAIN is an aquatic ecologist with a research focus on crayfish. He has spent his career working in the multitude of aquatic ecosystems throughout Louisiana, investigating the effects of physical and chemical habitat characteristics on various crayfish population characteristics, life history characteristics, and diversity of crayfishes throughout the state.

THAN BOVES is an associate professor of avian ecology at Arkansas State University. He has studied various aspects of ornithology involving ecology, behavior, evolution, and conservation of birds for nearly two decades. Much of his research has focused on New World warblers, but he has also researched barn owls, loggerhead shrikes, and avian forest communities.

JIM BULAK is a retired fisheries biologist who worked for the SCDNR.

JAY BUTFILOSKI is a certified wildlife biologist with the SCDNR. He is the statewide furbearer and alligator program coordinator, responsible for supervising the wildlife permitting office as well as management of all furbearer species in South Carolina and coordination of the statewide alligator hunting and nuisance programs. He has been with the SCDNR for more than nineteen years.

PEYTON CAGLE is a fisheries biologist with the Louisiana Department of Wildlife and Fisheries.

BRECK CARMICHAEL is a certified wildlife biologist employed by the SCDNR since 1985. Previously, he held the positions of assistant to the director, deputy director for the Wildlife and Freshwater Fisheries Division, and Statewide Small Game Project Supervisor. He is currently working primarily to further the goals of the South Carolina Bobwhite Initiative.

RICHARD CONNORS is a Nashville photographer and naturalist. He is former president of the Tennessee Ornithological Society and has worked as a biologist with the Tennessee State Parks, conducting surveys for their All Taxa Biodiversity Inventory. He has also been part of the U.S. Fish and Wildlife Service Breeding Bird Surveys and Partners in Flight point counts.

WARREN DOUGLAS is a ranger at Reelfoot Lake State Park in Tennessee. A graduate of the Univ. of Tennessee Martin, he is also a hunting and fishing guide.

CHRIS FISCHER is founding chairman and expedition leader of OCEARCH, which undertakes information-gathering voyages to do research on sharks.

BRYAN FRAZIER is a coastal shark biologist with the SCDNR.

WHIT GIBBONS is professor emeritus of ecology at the University of Georgia, where he taught herpetology and received the National Meritorious Teaching Award in herpetology. Whit wrote the original "Reptile and Amphibian Study" merit badge booklet for the Boy Scouts of America, has published more than 250 articles on herpetology and ecology in scientific journals, and is author of *Snakes of the Eastern United States.*

LEX GLOVER has been a wildlife technician with the SCDNR, in the Bird Conservation Program, for more than twenty-five years. Pursuing a career in wildlife, he was hired by SCDNR for seasonal work on the Breeding Bird Atlas Project and was later hired in a permanent position. He operates several bird banding stations and conducts surveys around the state, focusing on neotropical migrants.

NANCY HADLEY grew up on the South Carolina coast, where oyster reefs were a daily sight. In her thirty-five-year career with SCDNR, she studied mariculture, oyster ecology, and oyster reef restoration. She managed the state's shellfish program for the last decade of her career. In her retirement, she enjoys listening to the plentiful oysters visible from her deck.

RICK HAMRICK is a wildlife biologist with the Mississippi Department of Wildlife, Fisheries, and Parks (MDWFP). He is the Small Game and Habitat program leader and resides in Starkville. Rick grew up in East Central Mississippi and worked in wildlife research associate positions for the University of Georgia and Mississippi State University before joining MDWFP in 2007.

DR. GREG HARTMAN is a professor of biology at Gordon State College in Barnesville, Georgia. He received his master's degree from the University of Cincinnati and his Ph.D. from the University of New Mexico. He has taught courses about mammals and other vertebrates at several colleges and universities and has published numerous research articles and three book chapters on moles and their biology.

ANDY HERNDON is the Atlantic and shortnose sturgeon recovery coordinator for the National Oceanographic and Atmospheric Administration Fisheries in the Southeast. His work focuses on protecting sturgeon habitats and returning these animals to areas they used historically. Prior to working with sturgeon, he worked primarily on protecting endangered species from interactions with fishing gear.

JOE HEUBLEIN is currently the Gulf sturgeon recovery coordinator at National Oceanographic and Atmospheric Administration Fisheries in St. Petersburg, Florida. A native Californian, Joe studied fish at the University California, Davis, and San Francisco State University. He was the NOAA Fisheries green sturgeon recovery coordinator on the West Coast prior to moving to the Southeast.

DR. BILL HILTON JR. is executive director of the Hilton Pond Center for Piedmont Natural History in York, South Carolina. The mission of the Center is "to conserve plants, animals, habitats, and other natural components of the Piedmont Region of the eastern United States through observation, scientific study, and education for students of all ages." *Discover* magazine cited him as one of the "50 Best Brains in Science" and one of ten top amateur scientists in America.

JASON KAHN received his Ph.D. from West Virginia University for modeling abundance and survival of Atlantic sturgeon populations. He has worked with the National Marine Fisheries Service Office of Protected Resources since 2003 and has been the sturgeon specialist in their Headquarters' Interagency Cooperation Division since 2006. His current projects are analyzing Atlantic sturgeon genes, migrations, and reproductive success in the face of extreme weather events during spawning seasons.

DR. JOHN C. KILGO is a research wildlife biologist with the U.S. Department of Agriculture Forest Service Southern Research Station in New Ellenton, South Carolina. Although his research interests cover most vertebrate taxa, he has studied coyote ecology and the effects of coyotes on deer and other species at the U.S. Department of Energy's Savannah River Site and across the Southeast for the past fifteen years.

DENNIS KLEMM, Sea Turtle Recovery Coordinator–Southeast Regional Office, National Marine Fisheries Service, has worked on sea turtle issues since 2001, covering waters off North Carolina to Texas and the U.S. Caribbean. He is involved in all aspects of the Endangered Species Act as they relate to sea turtles.

"ROADKILL" GIL LACKEY is a freelance outdoor writer, editor, lecturer, and photographer from Nashville, Tennessee. He's an expert in the "How Not To" field, and he specializes in fictional outdoor humor stories. He's a naturalist and an outdoorsman who enjoys fly fishing, trail cameras, and all of the humor and wonder in the wilderness.

TIMOTHY MCCAY is a forest ecologist specializing in the biodiversity of the soil. He holds degrees in wildlife biology and ecology from the University of Florida, Penn State, and the University of Georgia. Tim currently teaches ecology and studies earthworms at Colgate University in upstate New York.

BILLY MCCORD was a full-time wildlife biologist, ecologist, and naturalist with SCDNR from 1978–2010. Much of his professional career through 2003 dealt with the study and management of migratory fish populations, and he was a member of national, state, and regional committees. Billy is currently a part-time natural history biologist with the SCDNR in Charleston. He has conducted research on migratory monarch butterflies since 1996, having tagged more than forty thousand monarchs, mostly in coastal South Carolina.

DR. CHRISTOPHER MAH is a research associate within the Department of Invertebrate Zoology at the National Museum of Natural History in Washington, D.C. He specializes in sea star diversity and evolution.

DR. CHRIS MAHER is a behavioral ecologist and a professor of biology at the University of Southern Maine. She earned a Ph.D. in animal behavior from the University of California, Davis; an M.S. in zoology from the University of Idaho; and a B.S. in zoology from Miami University. Since 1998, she has been conducting a long-term study of the ecology and behavior of woodchucks in southern Maine.

DON MANLEY is professor emeritus at Clemson University, where he was professor of entomology from 1978–2009. He earned his B.A. from UCLA, his M.A. from Cal State Long Beach, and his Ph.D. from the University of Arizona.

JOHN J. MARZLUFF is James W. Ridgeway Professor of Wildlife Science at the University of Washington. His graduate work at Northern Arizona University and initial postdoctoral research at the University of Vermont focused on the social behavior and ecology of jays and ravens. His current research focuses on the interactions of ravens and wolves in Yellowstone. Professor Marzluff has written five books and edited several others. He is a Fellow of the American Ornithologist's Union.

SALLY R. MURPHY was a wildlife biologist for SCDNR, where she created and ran the sea turtle program for thirty years. She was involved nationally as coleader of the first recovery sea turtle team and internationally as a member of the Wider Caribbean Sea Turtle Conservation Network. She has written or coauthored more than sixty scientific papers and popular articles, as well as a memoir, *Turning the Tide*.

TOM MURPHY is a non-game biologist with the SCDNR.

DAVID OSBORN was raised in rural Arkansas. After earning degrees in wildlife science from Arkansas Tech and Texas Tech, he worked as a wildlife biologist in Florida and Arkansas before joining, in 1993, the University of Georgia, where he serves as the deer research coordinator. David once was active in the sport of hunting squirrels with dogs, self-publishing the book *Squirrel Dog Basics*.

BILL POST is diadromous fishes coordinator with the SCDNR.

AL SEGARS is former stewardship coordinator at ACE Basin National Estuarine Research Reserve and veterinarian with the SCDNR. He has done extensive work with loggerhead sea turtles and manatees, has monitored shorebirds, studied fisheries, and worked on water contaminants. He was key to the naming of the Beaufort barrier islands as national and global Important Bird Areas by Audubon.

WILLIAM SHEAR is Trinkle Distinguished Professor Emeritus of Biology at Hampden-Sydney College. He specializes in the systematics and behavior of arachnids and myriapods.

JIM SPENCER is a retired biologist and wildlife manager from Arkansas and since the mid-1970s has been a prolific outdoor writer with credits in more than two hundred magazines. For much of his career, he was a writer/editor/public relations specialist for the Arkansas Game and Fish Commission. He has written five books on outdoor topics. He and his wife, outdoor writer Jill Easton, live in the north Arkansas Ozarks.

RITA VENABLE is the author of the field guide *Butterflies of Tennessee*. She was an assistant biologist with the Tennessee Department of Environment and Conservation, conducting biological surveys in state parks and natural areas with the All Taxa Biodiversity Inventory program. Rita currently lives in Franklin, Tennessee.

AMBER VON HARTEN is a fisheries specialist formerly with the South Carolina Sea Grant Extension Program.

RANDALL WELLS, director of the Sarasota Dolphin Research Program, has been studying dolphins, including bottlenose dolphins, since 1970. His primary focus is on how to reduce impacts of human activities on dolphins.

DR. ELIZABETH WENNER retired in 2010 as a senior marine scientist and program manager for Crustacean and Wetlands Research at the Marine Resources Center of the SCDNR. During her thirty-one-year tenure, she studied invertebrate communities in a variety of habitats from estuarine to deep sea. She also served as research coordinator for the ACE Basin National Estuarine Research Reserve and was principal investigator for the NOAA-funded SEAMAP program and the Southeastern Regional Taxonomic Center.

DAVID WHITAKER is a member of the South Atlantic Fishery Management Council. He retired from the SCDNR in 2018 after more than forty-one years of service, and retains an emeritus office. At retirement, he was serving as assistant deputy director at SCDNR in Charleston. He grew up in Americus, Georgia, and earned a degree in biology from Georgia Southwestern College and an M.S. in Marine Biology from the College of Charleston.

BRYANT WHITE is program manager of furbearer research and trapping policy for the Association of Fish and Wildlife Agencies, a position he has held since 2002. His primary focus is coordinating efforts to develop best management practices for trapping relative to the United States understanding with the European Union. He also engages with CITES, IUCN, and other domestic and international wildlife management groups on behalf of state fish and wildlife agencies. He has authored more than thirty publications on trapping, furbearer management, and human-wildlife conflict resolution.

J. D. WILLSON is an associate professor of biology at the University of Arkansas, Fayetteville. J. D.'s research focuses primarily on the population dynamics of reptiles and amphibians, especially those threatened by habitat alteration, pollution, and invasive species. He received his B.S. from Davidson College and Ph.D. from the University of Georgia's Savannah River Ecology Lab, where he studied the aquatic snakes in isolated wetlands.

Photography Credits

Phillip Jones, SCDNR staff photographer (retired) and South Carolina Wildlife photographer emeritus: American Crow (3), American Robin (33), Atlantic Horseshoe Crab (111), Bald Eagle (40), Black Rat Snake (56), Blue Jay (44), Bobcat (79), Bottlenose Dolphin (108), Bullfrog (59), Carpenter Bee (36), Coyote (89), Crayfish (115), Eastern Cottontail Rabbit (59), Eastern Oyster (131), Eastern Screech Owl (19), Groundhog (63), Loggerhead Sea Turtle (103), Luna Moth (30), Manatee (127), Monarch Butterfly (7), Pileated Woodpecker (27), Red Fox (69), Red Velvet Ant (87), Shrimp (99), Striped Bass (135), Wolf Spider (53)

Ted Borg, SCDNR staff photographer (retired): Common Whitetail Dragonfly (23), Eastern Gray Squirrel (49)

Lewis Rogers, SCDNR Wildlife Biologist (retired): Eastern Mole (72)

SCDNR Staff photo: Atlantic Sturgeon (122, Endangered Species Permit #16442)

Dan Garber, freelance photographer, 864-472-0698, 215 Dogwood Circle, Inman, SC, 29349: Earthworm (ii and 83), Ruby-Throated Hummingbird (12), Copperhead (75)

Courtesy OCEARCH: Great White Shark (138)

Courtesy Southeastern Regional Taxonomic Center: Starfish (118)

Courtesy University of Nebraska Department of Entomology: House Fly (16)

Index

Note: Boldface type designates the pages from the main chapter for each creature.

spiders, xi, xiii, 6, 14, 18, 21, 31, 45, 52–55, 96, 112
Spock, Mr., 111
squid, 109
squirrels, xi, 35, 43, 45, 49–52, 56, 57, 63, 68, 81, 149
  flying, 20, 28
Stanley, Henry Morton, x
starfish, 86, **117–121**, 133
Starfish Wasting Disease, 120
starlings, 20, 36, 82
Steamboat, Arizona, 89
Stevens, Bob, 136
St. Marys River, 122
Story of My Heart, The, xi
striped bass, **134–137**
  original or palmetto hybrid, 136
striped sea star, 119, 121
sumac, 32
sunfish family, 136
sunflower seeds, 44
Suwannee River, 122, 125
swallows, 28, 139
sweetgum, 30

tadpoles, 22, 97
Tampa Bay, 106, 123
Tennessee State Parks, 24, 39, 146
Tennessee Wildlife Resources Agency, 41
tent caterpillar, 14
Terres, John K., xi
termites, 19, 36, 84, 145
Texas, xiii, 9, 10, 11, 14, 30, 38, 58, 80, 87, 91, 100, 106, 112, 119, 126, 131 148, 149
Thibodaux, Louisiana, 115
Thoreau, Henry David, x, 45
Three Little Pigs, The, 78
Thumper, 59
ticks, 81, 91, 122
Tierra del Fuego, 112
timber rattlesnake, 76

titmice, 3, 44
toads, 31, 72, 84
tomatoes, 65, 75
tortoise, 59
Tractor Supply, 71
Travis, Randy, 33
tree frogs, 19, 45
Trichechus manatus, 130
  Caiman latirostris, 130
trumpet creeper, 13
tularemia, 62
tuna, 140
turkeys, xi, 39, 67, 68, 71
Turning the Tide: A Memoir, 103, 149
turtle excluder devices, 104
turtles, 84, 96, 102–107, 113, 116, 140, 149

U.N. General Assembly, 109
Upper Blackhead Reservoir, 137
U.S. Fish and Wildlife Service, 105, 117, 125, 129, 143, 146, 150
U.S. Forest Service, 90, 147
U.S. Geological Survey, 126, 145
U.S. Marine Mammal Protection Act, 109

Van Dyke, Henry, x
veery, 34
Velveteen Rabbit, the, 59
Venable, Rita, 29–32, 149
Vermont, 51, 148
Victoria, Australia, 59
Virginia, xiii, 53, 80, 105, 112, 116, 124, 131
voles, 20, 57, 68, 72, 76
Von Harten, Amber, 100–101, 149

Walmart, 67
walnut, 32, 139
walrus, 126, 140
warblers, 13, 26, 145
Washington, University of, 4, 5, 148
wasp, ix, 18, 31, 36, 86–88